Part 2

Rex Jones II

Java 4

Selenium
WebDriver

Come Learn
How To Program
For Automation Testing

This book only covers Java which is one of the programming languages for Selenium

Free Webinars, Videos, and Live Training

Mr. Jones plans to have **free** step-by-step demonstration webinars, videos, and live trainings walking people through concepts of Selenium and QTP/UFT from A - Z. The material will teach/train individuals the fundamentals of the programming language, fundamentals of Selenium and QTP/UFT, and important concepts of Selenium and QTP/UFT. All of the webinars, videos, and live training will be directed toward beginners as well as mid-level automation engineers.

Sign Up to Receive

1. 3 Tips To Master Selenium Within 30 Days
    http://tinyurl.com/3-Tips-For-Selenium

2. 3 Tips To Master QTP/UFT Within 30 Days
    http://tinyurl.com/3-Tips-For-QTP-UFT

3. Free Webinars, Videos, and Live Trainings
    http://tinyurl.com/Free-QTP-UFT-Selenium

Skype: rex.jones34
Twitter: @RexJonesII
Email: Rex.Jones@Test4Success.org
LinkedIn: https://www.linkedin.com/in/rexjones34

Rex Jones' Contact Information

Email Address: Rex.Jones@Test4Success.org
LinkedIn: https://www.linkedin.com/in/rexjones34
Books: http://tinyurl.com/Rex-Allen-Jones-Books
Twitter: @RexJonesII
Skype: rex.jones34

3 Tips To Master Selenium Within 30 Days
http://tinyurl.com/3-Tips-For-Selenium

Free Webinars, Videos, and Live Trainings
http://tinyurl.com/Free-QTP-UFT-Selenium

Table of Contents

Skype: rex.jones34
Twitter: @RexJonesII
Email: Rex.Jones@Test4Success.org
LinkedIn: https://www.linkedin.com/in/rexjones34

Table of Contents

3 Tips To Master Selenium Within 30 Days
http://tinyurl.com/3-Tips-For-Selenium

Free Webinars, Videos, and Live Trainings
http://tinyurl.com/Free-QTP-UFT-Selenium

Table of Contents

Skype: rex.jones34
Twitter: @RexJonesII
Email: Rex.Jones@Test4Success.org
LinkedIn: https://www.linkedin.com/in/rexjones34

Preface

According to TIOBE, Java is the most popular programming language within the programming community. Therefore Java is a great language to learn in the world of automating applications. A core set of Java is necessary to be effective on automation projects. *Part 2 – Java 4 Selenium WebDriver* provides a core set of Java plus concepts involving inheritance, packages, and much more.

Target Audience

The target audience is programmers with knowledge of variables, data types, operators, branches, and loops. It is recommended to read Part 1 – Java 4 Selenium WebDriver, if an individual needs to gain a foundation in Java.

Purpose

The purpose of this book is to not overwhelm you with hundreds and hundreds of pages (known as information overload) regarding Java. However it will provide valuable information that is concise with straightforward definitions, examples, and figures. After reading *Part 2 – Java 4 Selenium WebDriver,* a thorough understanding of Java and object-oriented programming will be in your possession.

3 Tips To Master Selenium Within 30 Days
http://tinyurl.com/3-Tips-For-Selenium

Free Webinars, Videos, and Live Trainings
http://tinyurl.com/Free-QTP-UFT-Selenium

About the Author

Rex Allen Jones II is a QA/Software Tester with a passion for sharing knowledge about testing software. He has been watching webinars, attending seminars, and testing applications over 10 years. Mr. Jones graduated from DeVry University with a Bachelor's of Science degree in Computer Information Systems (CIS).

Rex is an author, consultant, and former Board of Director for User Group: Dallas / Fort Worth Mercury User Group (DFWMUG) and member of User Group: Dallas / Fort Worth Quality Assurance Association (DFWQAA). In addition to his User Group memberships, he is a Certified Software Tester Engineer (CSTE) and has a Test Management Approach (TMap) certification.

Mr. Jones' advice for people interested in Automation Testing is to learn the programming language. This advice led him to write 4 programming books "(Part 1 & Part 2) You Must

Skype: rex.jones34
Twitter: @RexJonesII
Email: Rex.Jones@Test4Success.org
LinkedIn: https://www.linkedin.com/in/rexjones34

Learn VBScript for QTP/UFT" and "(Part 1 & Part 2) Java 4 Selenium WebDriver".
VBScript is the programming language for Unified Functional Testing (UFT) formerly
known as Quick Test Professional (QTP) and Java is one of the programming languages for
Selenium WebDriver.

In addition to the 4 programming books, Mr. Jones wrote 2 more books. The 5th book is
named Absolute Beginner (Part 1) Selenium WebDriver for Functional Automation Testing
which provides a deep foundation of Selenium WebDriver. Finally, a 6th book named Getting
Started With TestNG (A Java Test Framework). All books are available in Paperback,
eBook, and PDF.

3 Tips To Master Selenium Within 30 Days
http://tinyurl.com/3-Tips-For-Selenium

Free Webinars, Videos, and Live Trainings
http://tinyurl.com/Free-QTP-UFT-Selenium

Copyright, Legal Notice, and Disclaimer

ISBN-13: 978-1530867134
ISBN-10: 1530867134

Skype: rex.jones34
Twitter: @RexJonesII
Email: Rex.Jones@Test4Success.org
LinkedIn: https://www.linkedin.com/in/rexjones34

Acknowledgements

I would like to express my gratitude to my wife Tiffany, children Olivia Rexe' and Rex III, editor Samantha Mann, family, friends, and the many people who provided encouragement. Writing this book took time and your support helped pushed this book forward.

Thank You,

Rex Allen Jones II

Rex Allen Jones II

3 Tips To Master Selenium Within 30 Days
http://tinyurl.com/3-Tips-For-Selenium

Free Webinars, Videos, and Live Trainings
http://tinyurl.com/Free-QTP-UFT-Selenium

Videos

Building Blocks For Selenium

- (Part 1) Building Blocks For Selenium
  https://tinyurl.com/Selenium-Building-Blocks-Part1

- (Part 2) Building Blocks For Selenium
  https://tinyurl.com/Part2-Selenium-Building-Blocks

Java

- How To Install Selenium, Java, Eclipse, & TestNG
  https://tinyurl.com/Install-Selenium-Video

- Understanding Java Variables & Operators
  https://tinyurl.com/Variables-Operators-In-Java

Selenium

- Selenium Browser Methods
  https://tinyurl.com/BrowserMethods4Selenium

- Selenium WebElement Methods
  https://tinyurl.com/WebElementMethods4Selenium

Subscribe To Selenium 4 Beginners

- https://tinyurl.com/Subscribe-Selenium4Beginners

Skype: rex.jones34
Twitter: @RexJonesII
Email: Rex.Jones@Test4Success.org
LinkedIn: https://www.linkedin.com/in/rexjones34

Chapter 1
Introduction to Object-Oriented Programming

Structured programming is the programming paradigm prior to Object-Oriented Programming (OOP). The former paradigm is powerful but has limitations regarding large complex projects. As a result, Object-Oriented Programming (OOP) was developed to overcome limitations of structured programming. The effective concepts of structured programming plus new concepts birthed Object-Oriented Programming (OOP).

Object-Oriented Programming (OOP) is an approach centered on objects. As a result, creating objects is one of the most essential principles in OOP. All objects have two characteristics: state and behavior. State identifies the object and behavior represents the actions of the object.

Chapter 1 underlines Object-Oriented Programming (OOP) by providing an overview of this book "*Part 2 – Java 4 Selenium WebDriver*":

- ✓ Classes, Objects, and Methods
- ✓ Arrays and Strings
- ✓ Object-Oriented Programming (OOP)
- ✓ Packages
- ✓ Interfaces
- ✓ Errors, Exceptions, and Debugging
- ✓ Utilizing Input and Output

3 Tips To Master Selenium Within 30 Days
http://tinyurl.com/3-Tips-For-Selenium

Free Webinars, Videos, and Live Trainings
http://tinyurl.com/Free-QTP-UFT-Selenium

Chapter 1
Introduction to Object-Oriented Programming   (Part 2) Java 4 Selenium WebDriver

Classes, Objects, and Methods

Java is an object-oriented programming (OOP) language containing classes, objects, and methods (see *Classes, Objects, and Methods in Chapter 2*). A class is a blueprint for creating an object and a method execute a job for the object. Classes include data and code that operate on the data. Objects serve as the foundation for OOP while methods perform actions. A method's responsibility is to instruct the program what action to perform and how to perform the action.

Arrays and Strings

In Java, arrays and strings are objects (see *Arrays and Strings in Chapter 3*). An array is a group of related variables with the same data type, same name, and fixed number of values. All items in the array are accessed by an index which starts at zero. On the other hand, a string is a group of unchangeable characters. Many methods are available for strings that facilitate an operation on the object.

Object-Oriented Programming (OOP)

Object-Oriented Programming (OOP) is comprised of three concepts: inheritance, encapsulation, and polymorphism. Inheritance is a hierarchical concept which allows code and objects to be reused (see *Inheritance in Chapter 4*). Each class allows other classes to inherit its code. As a result, the relationship between the classes are superclass and subclass. Superclass is the parent class and subclass is the child class. The classes maintain a certain amount data in common while holding unique characteristics.

Encapsulation consists of data protection (see *Encapsulation in Chapter 4*). Protecting data prevents direct access from other parts of the program. Access is granted through access modifiers and accessor methods. Access modifiers place limitations on classes, variables, and methods while accessor methods set and return specific data.

Skype: rex.jones34
Twitter: @RexJonesII
Email: Rex.Jones@Test4Success.org
LinkedIn: https://www.linkedin.com/in/rexjones34

Chapter 1
Introduction to Object-Oriented Programming   (Part 2) Java 4 Selenium WebDriver

Polymorphism permits any number of methods to define its own implementation based on one interface (see *Polymorphism in Chapter 4*). This concept helps evolve Object-Oriented Programming (OOP). A superclass contains the method's structure while a subclass determines how to implement the structure.

Packages

A package is a collection of related classes (see *Packages in Chapter 5*). The package is comparable to a folder and the classes are similar to files within the folder. Each class within the package can be accessed by the package name. It is important to know that a package must be imported if a class wants to use members from a different class.

Interfaces

An interface is a collection of related methods (see *Interfaces in Chapter 6*). Generally, most interfaces do not include the body of a method. Therefore an interface method reveals what action to perform but not how to perform the action. This concept allows a class to implement the interface method and decide how to perform the action. Each class has the ability to implement a different action for the same interface method.

Errors, Exceptions, and Debugging

Errors are unavoidable problems in a program. New programmers as well as experienced programmers will face errors. Syntax, runtime, and logical are three types of errors in Java. Syntax errors stop the code from executing while runtime errors allow code to execute then generate an error. Logical errors are the most difficult errors to detect due to no error message during execution. The programmer must know what to expect in order to find and resolve a logical error.

3 Tips To Master Selenium Within 30 Days
http://tinyurl.com/3-Tips-For-Selenium

Free Webinars, Videos, and Live Trainings
http://tinyurl.com/Free-QTP-UFT-Selenium

Chapter 1
Introduction to Object-Oriented Programming   (Part 2) Java 4 Selenium WebDriver
An exception is an error that occurs at runtime. This type of error can be managed by a block of code called an exception handler. Exception handlers allow the program to generate an error but continue executing after the error. Debugging is a process that allows a programmer to observe then correct an error and/or exception. A tool called debugger simplifies the task of resolving errors due to breakpoints and its step-by-step features.

Note: See *Errors, Exceptions, and Debugging in Chapter 7* for more information

Utilizing Input and Output

Java's Input and Output (I/O) is a very large system consisting of many classes, interfaces, and methods (see *Utilizing Input and Output in Chapter 8*). Information is read from an input source and written to an output destination. The programs perform input and output through streams whereby streams represent data. Files in Java are stored and organized for convenience. Most of the files are structured in a hierarchy known as a tree. At the top of every tree is the root node which contains folders and files. All folders and files have a distinctive path within the tree. The files can be created, deleted, moved, copied, and verified for existence.

Chapter 1 provided an overview of the upcoming chapters. The subsequent chapters explore classes, objects, methods, arrays, strings, inheritance, packages, interfaces, errors, exceptions, debugging, and Java's input/output system. Chapter 2 will thoroughly explain classes, objects, and methods which is the cornerstone of object-oriented programming.

Skype: rex.jones34
Twitter: @RexJonesII
Email: Rex.Jones@Test4Success.org
LinkedIn: https://www.linkedin.com/in/rexjones34

Chapter 2
Classes, Objects, and Methods

Object-oriented programming (OOP) is a programming language structured around objects. Classes, objects, and methods are interrelated fundamentals within OOP. An <u>object</u> is anything that can be seen or perceived. However, a <u>class</u> is a template for <u>objects</u> while a <u>methods</u> provide interaction with a <u>class</u> from various components of the program.

The data and the code (known as statements) that operate on the data are two merged notions of an object. As a result, the two merged notions allow a concept called information hiding whereby data can be hidden. Therefore by default an object's data can be accessed only by methods holding the object. The limited access prevent other program components from interfering and causing errors. If another component wants to change an object's data then the component must call a publicly accessible method. The following are four types of methods:

1. <u>Instance</u> – A method that can be accessed by objects
2. <u>Class</u> – A method shared between all objects in a class
3. <u>Main</u> – A special method used to run an application. This type of method is not needed for Selenium WebDriver.
4. <u>Constructor</u> – A special method used to initialize objects of a particular class

Methods and variables are labeled members of a class since they form the class. Access to both members are controlled by four modifiers:

1. public – A modifier that allows access to code defined outside of its <u>class</u>
2. private – A modifier that allows access to other members within its <u>class</u>
3. no modifier – A modifier that allows access to all <u>classes</u> within its <u>package</u>
4. protected – A modifier that allows access within its <u>package</u> and to all <u>subclasses</u>

3 Tips To Master Selenium Within 30 Days
http://tinyurl.com/3-Tips-For-Selenium

Free Webinars, Videos, and Live Trainings
http://tinyurl.com/Free-QTP-UFT-Selenium

Chapter 2
Classes, Objects, and Methods   (Part 2) Java 4 Selenium WebDriver

Usually, members of a class are accessed by objects within its own class. However, the keyword "static" permits a member to be accessed before any object is created within its class. Methods and variables are declared static when the keyword is placed in front of the member.

Chapter two will explain the following regarding classes, objects, and methods:

- ✓ Classes
- ✓ Objects
- ✓ Methods
- ✓ This Keyword
- ✓ Annotations
- ✓ Access Modifiers
- ✓ Static Keyword

Classes

Classes define data and code that operates on the data. The data is represented by variables while the code is represented by methods. Both variables and methods are members of a class. Hence a class is a template that defines the structure of an object. Therefore the structure of a class must be precise. Classes formed with one logical entity makes the class complete. It is important to define classes with information that is logically connected. For example, a class that contains information about an English class would not contain unrelated information about the school zone speed limit.

Most real-world classes include an instance variable and a method to operate on the instance variable. Remember from the first book *"(Part 1) Absolute Beginner: Java 4 Selenium WebDriver"* an instance variable is declared inside a class but outside of a method. As a result, values of an instance variable are unique to each object. This type of variable can be used before or after it is initialized with visibility to all methods within a class. The following is the syntax for defining a class:

Skype: rex.jones34
Twitter: @RexJonesII
Email: Rex.Jones@Test4Success.org
LinkedIn: https://www.linkedin.com/in/rexjones34

Chapter 2
Classes, Objects, and Methods   (Part 2) Java 4 Selenium WebDriver
Syntax
class ClassName

```
{
        // Declare Instance Variable
        variableType variableName1;
        variableType variableName2;
        variableType variableNameN;

        // Declare Methods
        methodType methodName1 ()
        {
                // Body of the Method
        }

        methodType methodName2 ()
        {
                // Body of the Method
        }

        methodType methodNameN ()
        {
                // Body of the Method
        }
}
```

The following is an example of a data only class called English which stores three instance variables: students, weeks, and days.

3 Tips To Master Selenium Within 30 Days
http://tinyurl.com/3-Tips-For-Selenium

Free Webinars, Videos, and Live Trainings
http://tinyurl.com/Free-QTP-UFT-Selenium

Chapter 2
Classes, Objects, and Methods   (Part 2) Java 4 Selenium WebDriver

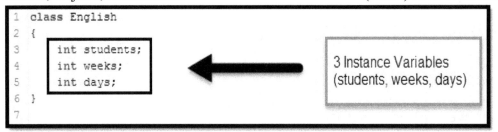

Figure 2.1 – Data Only Class

Line 1 defines the English class and lines 3 – 5 declare the instance variables. English is a school course while instance variable students represent the number of students in the class, weeks represent the number of weeks for the English course, and days represent the number of days per week. Whenever a class is defined, it is considered a new data type. In this case, the new data type "English" is the class name.

Note: A convention for naming classes is to use an UpperCamelCase where each word in the class name begins with a capital letter (i.e., EnglishCourse).

Objects

Object-Oriented programming (OOP) is built upon objects. Therefore it is crucial to understand how objects are formed and utilized. An object can be anything. All objects share two characteristics: state and behavior. State identifies the object and behavior represent the actions of the object. For example, a dog has a state (name, breed, color) which identifies the dog and behavior (bark, jump, fetch) which represent the dog's actions. The state of an object is supported by variables while behavior is implemented through methods. Objects are created using the keyword "new". The following example illustrates how to create an object and how to access instance variables:

Skype: rex.jones34
Twitter: @RexJonesII
Email: Rex.Jones@Test4Success.org
LinkedIn: https://www.linkedin.com/in/rexjones34

Chapter 2
Classes, Objects, and Methods   (Part 2) Java 4 Selenium WebDriver

```
1  class English
2  {
3      int students;
4      int weeks;
5      int days;
6  }
7
8  class OneEnglishCourse
9  {
10     public static void main (String args[])
11     {
12         English ENG101 = new English ();
13         int totalDays;
14
15         ENG101.students = 10;
16         ENG101.weeks = 4;
17         ENG101.days = 3;
18
19         totalDays = ENG101.weeks * ENG101.days;
20         System.out.println("The English 101 course is a total of " + totalDays + " days");
21     }
22 }
```

Create an object using the keyword new

Access the instance variables using the dot (.) operator

Figure 2.2 – Create New Object and Access Instance Variables

Program Output:
The English 101 course is a total of 12 days

Line 12 creates a new object (English ENG101 = new English ();) by combining two steps. According to Java A Beginner's Guide Sixth Edition (2014), the two steps combined can be rewritten like the following to show each step individually (page 106):

1. **English ENG101;** - The left side of the assignment which declares a variable called ENG101 of class type English
2. **ENG101 = new English ();** - The right side of the assignment which creates a copy of the object and give ENG101 a reference to the object

3 Tips To Master Selenium Within 30 Days
http://tinyurl.com/3-Tips-For-Selenium

Free Webinars, Videos, and Live Trainings
http://tinyurl.com/Free-QTP-UFT-Selenium

Chapter 2
Classes, Objects, and Methods   (Part 2) Java 4 Selenium WebDriver
ENG101 is a creation (known as instance) of English after creating the new object. Lines 15 – 17 assign values to the instance variables by accessing the variables using the dot (.) operator. The following is the syntax for utilizing the dot operator:

Syntax
objectName.MemberName;

The dot operator connects an object with a member (instance variable or method). In this example, an object name (ENG101) is located on the left and the instance variables (students, weeks, days) are located on the right. An object hold its own instance variable copy defined by the class. Therefore, if multiple objects exist, each object can hold a different value than the other object. The following example illustrate a creation of two objects (ENG101 and ENG202):

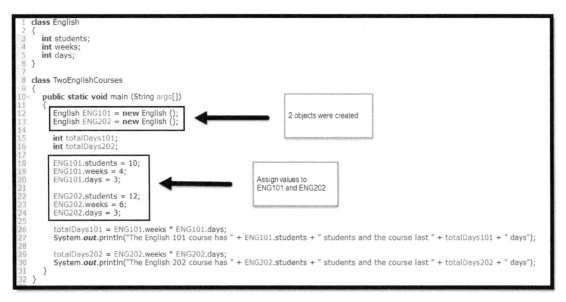

Figure 2.3 – Two Objects Created

Skype: rex.jones34
Twitter: @RexJonesII
Email: Rex.Jones@Test4Success.org
LinkedIn: https://www.linkedin.com/in/rexjones34

Chapter 2
Classes, Objects, and Methods   (Part 2) Java 4 Selenium WebDriver
Program Output:

```
The English 101 course has 10 students and the course last 12 days
The English 202 course has 12 students and the course last 18 days
```

Lines 12 and 13 create two objects (ENG101 and ENG202) then assign values to both objects in lines 18 – 24. Recall, if multiple objects exist then each object can hold a different value than the other object. In this example, a different value is assigned to variables "students and weeks" but variable "days" contains the same value "3" for both objects.

Note: The convention for variables are lowerCamelCase where each word in the variable name begins with a capital letter except the first word. However, ENG101 and ENG202 is an exception which contains all capital letters because school courses normally have all capital letters before a number in their course name.

Methods

A method is a block of code surrounded by curly brackets that perform a specific action/task. The purpose is to manipulate and provide access to data defined by the class. In other words, a method performs actions on the data. It is best for all methods to carry out a single task. For example, a good method will only perform a single task of adding numbers but not adding numbers and saving data to a file. The program may become difficult to read and understand if a method carries out more than one task.

Methods consist of a header and body. The method header includes a method type and a method name. The convention for method name is similar to a variable name which consist of a lowerCamelCase style. Each word begins with a capital letter except the first word. Succeeding the method name is a required pair of parenthesis which sets apart variables from methods. The following is the syntax for method:

3 Tips To Master Selenium Within 30 Days
http://tinyurl.com/3-Tips-For-Selenium

Free Webinars, Videos, and Live Trainings
http://tinyurl.com/Free-QTP-UFT-Selenium

Chapter 2
Classes, Objects, and Methods   (Part 2) Java 4 Selenium WebDriver
Syntax
methodType methodName (parameter-list)
{
        // Method Body
}

The methodType (known as return type) determines the data type returned by the method. A programmer is forced to use keyword "void" for the methodType if no values are returned. The methodName can be any name except a Java keyword. A good technique to employ for naming a method is verb-noun combinations, such as "getOrder or addNumbers". Method body is where code will be executed to carry out a task. The parameter list are variables that receive arguments passed to the method. If the method has no parameters then the parameter list must remain empty.

Note: A method signature is the methodName and parameter list.

Method Returns
Method returns are concepts that return a value from a method or transfer control out of a method. Both concepts are achieved by using the return keyword. Execution is terminated and subsequent statements within the method are skipped no matter where the return keyword is located. The following are two method return types:

1. Methods that return a value
2. Methods that cannot return a value

According to ORACLE, a method returns to the code that invoked it when it

- completes all the statements in the method,
- reaches a return statement or
- throws an exception

whichever occurs first.

Skype: rex.jones34
Twitter: @RexJonesII
Email: Rex.Jones@Test4Success.org
LinkedIn: https://www.linkedin.com/in/rexjones34

Chapter 2
Classes, Objects, and Methods   (Part 2) Java 4 Selenium WebDriver

<u>Note</u>: Usually, the return keyword (also known as return statement) is not used for methods that cannot return a value. It is not used because all of the code within the method is completed before executing the return keyword. However, if the return keyword is used, then it will be implemented at the end of the method to transfer control.

Return A Value

Most methods return a value which specifies the outcome of a calculation or result (pass, fail, etc.) The return value is required to be the same data type as the method type. For instance, if the method type is an "int" data type then the return type must be an "int" data type. The following is a syntax and example for a method return:

Syntax
return value;

Chapter 2
Classes, Objects, and Methods

```
1   class English
2   {
3       int students, weeks, days;          2
4
5       int totalDays ()
6       {
7           return weeks * days;
8       }
9   }
10
11  class TwoEnglishCourses
12  {
13      public static void main (String args[])
14      {
15          English ENG101 = new English ();
16          English ENG202 = new English ();
17
18          ENG101.students = 10;
19          ENG101.weeks = 4;
20          ENG101.days = 3;
21
22          ENG202.students = 12;
23          ENG202.weeks = 6;
24          ENG202.days = 3;
25
26          System.out.println("The English 101 course has " + ENG101.students + " students and the course last " + ENG101.totalDays () + " days");
27          System.out.println("The English 202 course has " + ENG202.students + " students and the course last " + ENG202.totalDays () + " days");
28      }
29  }
```

This method "**int totalDays ()**" returns the total number of days for an English course

Both statements "**ENG101.totalDays ()**" and "**ENG202.totalDays ()**" call method totalDays () then retrieves the total number of days from method

Figure 2.4 – Return a Value

Program Output:
```
The English 101 course has 10 students and the course last 12 days
The English 202 course has 12 students and the course last 18 days
```

Methods return a value to the code that called the method. In this example, lines 26 and 27 make calls to the method (int totalDays ()) at line 5. Then the method returns the outcome from calculation (weeks * days) back to lines 26 and 27. The dot (.) operator connects both objects (ENG101 and ENG202) to a member (totalDays ()) which is a method. The method is placed on the right side of the dot operator while the objects are located on the left:

Skype: rex.jones34
Twitter: @RexJonesII
Email: Rex.Jones@Test4Success.org
LinkedIn: https://www.linkedin.com/in/rexjones34

Chapter 2
Classes, Objects, and Methods   (Part 2) Java 4 Selenium WebDriver
ENG101.totalDays ();
ENG202.totalDays ();

Line 3 declares all instance variables as an "int" data type. Therefore the instance variables (weeks and days) used for calculation at line 7 is automatically declared with an "int" data type. This will not cause a return error because the return type (line 7) and method type (line 5) possess the same data type. The values for each instance variable are calculated based on lines 19, 20, 23, and 24. Lines 19 and 23 contain values for variable "weeks" while lines 20 and 24 contain values for variable "days".

Return No Value

Methods that cannot return a value are called void methods. The keyword "void" is implemented as the methodType rather than a data type such as "int". An error occurs if there is an attempt to return a value from the void method. The following is a void method example:

3 Tips To Master Selenium Within 30 Days
http://tinyurl.com/3-Tips-For-Selenium

Free Webinars, Videos, and Live Trainings
http://tinyurl.com/Free-QTP-UFT-Selenium

Chapter 2
Classes, Objects, and Methods   (Part 2) Java 4 Selenium WebDriver

```
1   class English
2   {
3       int students, weeks, days;
4
5       void totalDays ()
6       {
7           System.out.println(weeks * days);
8       }
9   }
10
11  class TwoEnglishCourses
12  {
13      public static void main (String args[])
14      {
15          English ENG101 = new English ();
16          English ENG202 = new English ();
17
18          ENG101.students = 10;
19          ENG101.weeks = 4;
20          ENG101.days = 3;
21
22          ENG202.students = 12;
23          ENG202.weeks = 6;
24          ENG202.days = 3;
25
26          System.out.println("How many students are in the English 101 course? " + ENG101.students);
27          System.out.println("The course is " + ENG101.days + " days for " + ENG101.weeks + " weeks.");
28          System.out.print("Therefore the course last the following total number of days:");
29          ENG101.totalDays();
30          System.out.println("\n");
31
32          System.out.println("How many students are in the English 202 course? " + ENG202.students);
33          System.out.println("The course is " + ENG202.days + " days for " + ENG202.weeks + " weeks.");
34          System.out.print("Therefore the course last the following total number of days:");
35          ENG202.totalDays();
36      }
37  }
```

Void method **totalDays ()** prints the total number of days from expression **(weeks * days)**

Figure 2.5 – Void Method

Program Output:

```
How many students are in the English 101 course? 10
The course is 3 days for 4 weeks.
Therefore the course last the following total number of days: 12


How many students are in the English 202 course? 12
The course is 3 days for 6 weeks.
Therefore the course last the following total number of days: 18
```

Line 5 displays keyword "void" which indicates the method will not return any values.
Nevertheless, the void method only performs a task of calculating the total of number of

Skype: rex.jones34
Twitter: @RexJonesII
Email: Rex.Jones@Test4Success.org
LinkedIn: https://www.linkedin.com/in/rexjones34

Chapter 2
Classes, Objects, and Methods   (Part 2) Java 4 Selenium WebDriver

days. Line 7 prints the total days after multiplying weeks and days. The following displays an error when the <u>void</u> method implements the return keyword with a value:

```
 1   class English
 2   {
 3       int students, weeks, days;
 4
 5       // A void method cannot return a value
 6       void totalDays ()
 7       {
 8           return weeks * days
 9       }
10   }
```

Figure 2.6 – Void Method Error

Pass Arguments To Parameters

Arguments are values passed to a method while parameters receives the values. In other words, parameters receive arguments. Parameter variables are declared within a method's parenthesis and operate like a local variable. Local variables and parameter variables are only visible to the method where is declared. It is important to know that one or more arguments can be passed to individual parameters. The following is an example of passing two arguments to two parameters:

3 Tips To Master Selenium Within 30 Days
http://tinyurl.com/3-Tips-For-Selenium

Free Webinars, Videos, and Live Trainings
http://tinyurl.com/Free-QTP-UFT-Selenium

Chapter 2
Classes, Objects, and Methods   (Part 2) Java 4 Selenium WebDriver

```
 1  class English
 2  {
 3ⁿ     int totalDays (int wk, int d)
 4      {
 5          return wk * d;
 6      }
 7  }
 8
 9  class TwoEnglishCourses
10  {
11ⁿ     public static void main (String args[])
12      {
13          English ENG101 = new English ();
14          English ENG202 = new English ();
15
16          System.out.println("The English 101 course is a total of " + ENG101.totalDays (4, 3) + " days");
17          System.out.println("The English 202 course is a total of " + ENG202.totalDays (6, 3) + " days");
18      }
19  }
```

Arguments "**4, 3**" and "**6, 3**" are passed to parameters "**wk, d**"

Figure 2.7 – Pass Arguments To Parameters

Program Output:
```
The English 101 course is a total of 12 days
The English 202 course is a total of 18 days
```

- Line 3 defines two parameters "wk, d" for method totalDays (). Methods can have more than one parameter by separating each parameter with a comma
- Lines 16 and 17 indicates the arguments "4, 3" for object "ENG101" and "6, 3" for object "ENG202" are passed to parameters "wk, d"

Note: Objects can be passed to a method and returned from a method.

Method Types
The following are the four types of methods:

Skype: rex.jones34
Twitter: @RexJonesII
Email: Rex.Jones@Test4Success.org
LinkedIn: https://www.linkedin.com/in/rexjones34

Chapter 2
Classes, Objects, and Methods   (Part 2) Java 4 Selenium WebDriver

Instance Methods

Instance methods are called (known as invoked) by using an object. Therefore an instance method is similar to an instance variable whereby both members can be accessed through initialized objects. However, instance variables can be accessed with an object reference or without an object reference. The following is an instance method example:

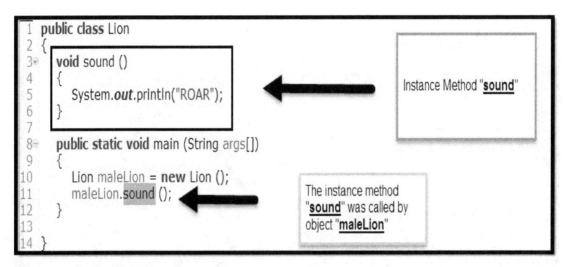

```
1   public class Lion
2   {
3       void sound ()
4       {
5           System.out.println("ROAR");
6       }
7
8       public static void main (String args[])
9       {
10          Lion maleLion = new Lion ();
11          maleLion.sound ();
12      }
13
14  }
```

Instance Method "**sound**"

The instance method "**sound**" was called by object "**maleLion**"

Figure 2.8   Instance Method

Program Output:
ROAR

- Lines 3 – 6 starts and completes the instance method "sound"
- Line 10 creates an object "maleLion" using keyword "new"

3 Tips To Master Selenium Within 30 Days
http://tinyurl.com/3-Tips-For-Selenium

Free Webinars, Videos, and Live Trainings
http://tinyurl.com/Free-QTP-UFT-Selenium

Chapter 2
Classes, Objects, and Methods   (Part 2) Java 4 Selenium WebDriver

- Line 11 calls the instance method "sound" through initialized object "maleLion"

Class Methods

A class method (known as static method) is similar to a class variable whereby they are declared with a static keyword. The static keyword means the member belongs to the class and shared between all objects. Class methods can be accessed via the object name or class name. However, a warning appears when accessing the method by an object. Therefore the favored way to access classed methods is through class name. The following is a class method example:

```
1  class StaticAddNumbers
2  {
3      static int a, b;
4
5      static int addNumbers ()
6      {
7          return a + b;
8      }
9  }
10
11 class StaticExample
12 {
13     public static void main(String[] args)
14     {
15         StaticAddNumbers objAdd = new StaticAddNumbers ();
16
17         objAdd.a = 20;
18         StaticAddNumbers.b = 30;
19
20         System.out.println("The addition of variables 'a + b' is " + objAdd.addNumbers() + " and accessed by an object");
21         System.out.println("The addition of variables 'a + b' is " + StaticAddNumbers.addNumbers() + " and accessed by a class name");
22     }
23 }
```

The static variables are "**a, b**" and static method is "**addNumbers**"

The static method "**addNumbers**" is called by an object name "**objAdd**" and class name "**StaticAddNumbers**"

Figure 2.9 – Class Method

Program Output:
```
The addition of variables 'a + b' is 50 and accessed by an object
The addition of variables 'a + b' is 50 and accessed by a class name
```

Skype: rex.jones34
Twitter: @RexJonesII
Email: Rex.Jones@Test4Success.org
LinkedIn: https://www.linkedin.com/in/rexjones34

Chapter 2
Classes, Objects, and Methods   (Part 2) Java 4 Selenium WebDriver

- Line 3 declares two class/static variables "a, b"
- Lines 5 – 7 defines the class/static method "addNumbers"
- Line 17 assigns 20 to class variable "a". Notice, the warning next to line 17 that states "The static field StaticAddNumbers.a should be accessed in a static way". This warning means the class variable (known as static variable) is preferred to be accessed by class name. Line 18 does not have a warning because class name precedes the variable name "b"
- Line 20 is similar to line 18. A warning message appears because the static method is accessed via object name rather than class name "i.e., line 21"

Note: Class methods can only access class variables and only call other class methods.

Main Method
The main method is unique and mandatory if a particular class begins the program. This method is required because it executes the program. The following is the syntax for main method:

Syntax
public static void main(String[] args)
{
        // Method Body
}

There are several examples of the main method but the following explains each component:

- public - the method can be accessed by all classes
- static – the method is shared between all objects
- void – the method does not return any values
- String[] args – the method receives a String argument and pass the argument to the program

3 Tips To Master Selenium Within 30 Days
http://tinyurl.com/3-Tips-For-Selenium

Free Webinars, Videos, and Live Trainings
http://tinyurl.com/Free-QTP-UFT-Selenium

Chapter 2
Classes, Objects, and Methods   (Part 2) Java 4 Selenium WebDriver

Note: The main method is explained in this chapter because *Part 2 – Java 4 Selenium WebDriver* focuses on Java programming. However, Selenium WebDriver write simple checks uses a testing framework such as JUnit and TestNG that will not require the main method. The next book "*Selenium WebDriver for Functional Automation Testing*" will focus on Selenium and dive into JUnit and TestNG.

Constructors

A constructor is a special method that has the same name as the class. If a constructor is not defined then a blank constructor is automatically created. Consequently all classes contain a constructor which initialize objects of a specific class. A new object calls a constructor every time the object is created. By default, the instance variables are initialized to zero for numeric types, null for reference types, and false for boolean types.

Constructors have the ability to set the initial value for an instance variable. Recall an instance variable can be accessed and assigned a value using the dot operator. In Figure 2.4 – Return A Value, the following instance variables were assigned values:

ENG101.students = 10;
ENG101.weeks = 4;
ENG101.days = 3;

ENG202.students = 12;
ENG202.weeks = 6;
ENG202.days = 3;

Constructors contain parameters which receive arguments when an object is created. The following example illustrates how to pass arguments to a constructor:

Skype: rex.jones34
Twitter: @RexJonesII
Email: Rex.Jones@Test4Success.org
LinkedIn: https://www.linkedin.com/in/rexjones34

Chapter 2
Classes, Objects, and Methods   (Part 2) Java 4 Selenium WebDriver

```
1  class English
2  {
3      int students, weeks, days;
4
5      English (int s, int w, int d)
6      {
7          students = s;
8          weeks = w;
9          days = d;
10     }
11
12     int totalDays ()
13     {
14         return weeks * days;
15     }
16 }
17
18 class TwoEnglishCourses
19 {
20     public static void main (String args[])
21     {
22         English ENG101 = new English (10, 4, 3);
23         English ENG202 = new English (12, 6, 3);
24
25         System.out.println("The English 101 course has " + ENG101.students + " students and the course last " + ENG101.totalDays () + " days");
26         System.out.println("The English 202 course has " + ENG202.students + " students and the course last " + ENG202.totalDays () + " days");
27     }
28 }
```

The constructor "**English**" defines 3 parameters "**s, w, l**"

The values are used to initialize the instance variables students, weeks, and days

Figure 2.10 – Parameterized Constructor

Program Output:
```
The English 101 course has 10 students and the course last 12 days
The English 202 course has 12 students and the course last 18 days
```

Line 5 – 10 create a constructor which defines three parameters "s, w, d" on line 5. Each parameter is used to initialize the instance variables "students, weeks, days" on lines 7 - 9. After lines 22 and 23 are executed, the values "10, 4, 3" for ENG101 and values "12, 6, 3" for ENG202 are assigned to the parameters "s, w, d". As a result, the values are passed to the English () constructor when the keyword "new" creates each object "ENG101 and ENG202".

3 Tips To Master Selenium Within 30 Days
http://tinyurl.com/3-Tips-For-Selenium

Free Webinars, Videos, and Live Trainings
http://tinyurl.com/Free-QTP-UFT-Selenium

Chapter 2
Classes, Objects, and Methods   (Part 2) Java 4 Selenium WebDriver
<u>Note</u>: Constructors are not defined with a method type such as int or <u>void</u>. Notice how line 5 begins with English then define the parameters. Java allows a class to contain multiple constructors. The feature is called constructor overloading if the constructors contain a different parameter list.

This Keyword

The word "this" is a keyword which operates as a reference inside <u>instance methods</u> and/or <u>constructors</u>. It refers to the current object or member of the current object whose method is being called. The keyword "this" is optional but useful when a programmer decides to hide information. In addition, the keyword "this" prevents uncertainty in a program when a local variable and instance variable contain the same name. A warning message states "The assignment to variable name has no effect" if both variables have the same name. The following example shows how to use keyword "this" when the local variable and instance variable contain the same name:

Skype: rex.jones34
Twitter: @RexJonesII
Email: Rex.Jones@Test4Success.org
LinkedIn: https://www.linkedin.com/in/rexjones34

Chapter 2
Classes, Objects, and Methods   (Part 2) Java 4 Selenium WebDriver

```java
 1  public class ThisKeyword
 2  {
 3      int testVariable = 34;
 4
 5      void hideInstanceVariable ()
 6      {
 7          int testVariable = 15;
 8
 9          System.out.println("What is the value of the local variable NOT using the keyword 'this'? " + testVariable);
10          System.out.println("What is the value of the instance variable using the keyword 'this'? " + this.testVariable);
11      }
12
13      public static void main(String[] args)
14      {
15          ThisKeyword objHide = new ThisKeyword ();
16
17          objHide.hideInstanceVariable ();
18      }
19  }
```

Local Variable = testVariable

Instance Variable = this.testVariable

Figure 2.11 – This Keyword

Program Output:
```
What is the value of the local variable NOT using the keyword 'this'? 15
What is the value of the instance variable using the keyword 'this'? 34
```

- Line 3 declares and initializes an instance variriable "testVariable" to a value of 34
- Line 7 declares and initializes a local variable "testVariable" to a value of 15
- Line 9 print a message which includes the local variable "testVariable"
- Line 10 prints a message which includes the instance variable "this.testVariable" using the keyword "this"

Annotations

According to dictionary.com, annotation means, "a critical or explanatory note." Recall from *Part 1 – Java 4 Selenium WebDriver*, comments are notes that help programmers understand the program. An annotation is similar to a comment whereby they both provide information.

3 Tips To Master Selenium Within 30 Days
http://tinyurl.com/3-Tips-For-Selenium

Free Webinars, Videos, and Live Trainings
http://tinyurl.com/Free-QTP-UFT-Selenium

Chapter 2
Classes, Objects, and Methods   (Part 2) Java 4 Selenium WebDriver

However, comments are ignored by the compiler while annotations supply data to the compiler. Annotations provide metadata which is data that describes data.

All annotations start with an at "@" symbol and specify the purpose of a method. Some annotations can be customized to replace comments and predefined annotations such as @Override. The following are examples of three TestNG annotations used in Selenium WebDriver:

1. @BeforeTest – execute one time before the first Test Method
2. @Test – set a Java method as a Test Method
3. @AfterTest – execute one time after the last Test Method

Note: Annotations are illustrated and explained in the Getting Started With TestNG book.

Static Keyword

The static keyword can be applied to variables, methods, blocks, and nested classes. Usually, the members of a class are accessed through an object of the class via the dot operator. When a member is declared as static, the member can be accessed prior to creating an object. However to access a static member, it is best to precede the static member with a class name and dot operator rather than the object name and dot operator. A warning message appears if the static member is preceded by an object name and dot operator. The following is the syntax and example of a static variable:

Syntax
ClassName.variableName;

Skype: rex.jones34
Twitter: @RexJonesII
Email: Rex.Jones@Test4Success.org
LinkedIn: https://www.linkedin.com/in/rexjones34

Chapter 2
Classes, Objects, and Methods   (Part 2) Java 4 Selenium WebDriver

```
1   class StaticAddNumbers
2   {
3       static int a;                    Class Name = StaticAddNumbers
4       int b;                           Static Variable = a
5
6       int addNumbers ()
7       {
8           return a + b;
9       }
10  }
11
12  class StaticExample
13  {
14      public static void main(String[] args)          The static variable is accessed by using
15      {                                                the ClassName.variableName
16          StaticAddNumbers objAdd = new StaticAddNumbers ();   "StaticAddNumbers.a"
17
18          objAdd.b = 50;
19          StaticAddNumbers.a = 25;
20
21          System.out.println("The value of 'objAdd.b' is " + objAdd.b);
22          System.out.println("The value of 'a' is " + StaticAddNumbers.a);
23          System.out.println("The total of 'a + b' is " + objAdd.addNumbers() + "\n");
24
25          StaticAddNumbers.a = 30;
26          System.out.println("The value of 'a' changed to " + StaticAddNumbers.a + " but the value of 'objAdd.b' remains " + objAdd.b);
27          System.out.println("The total of 'a+b' is " + + objAdd.addNumbers());
28      }
29  }
```

Figure 2.12 – Static Variable

Program Output:
```
The value of 'objAdd.b' is 50
The value of 'a' is 25
The total of 'a + b' is 75

The value of 'a' changed to 30 but the value of 'objAdd.b' remains 50
The total of 'a+b' is 80
```

Line 3 declares a static variable named "a" within class "StaticAddNumbers". The variable "a" is accessed in lines 19, 22, 25, and 26 by using the class name, dot operator, and static variable name. Lines 19 and 25 set the value while lines 22 and 26 displays the value. Static variables are treated like global variables and initialized at the start of execution.

3 Tips To Master Selenium Within 30 Days
http://tinyurl.com/3-Tips-For-Selenium

Free Webinars, Videos, and Live Trainings
http://tinyurl.com/Free-QTP-UFT-Selenium

Chapter 2
Classes, Objects, and Methods   (Part 2) Java 4 Selenium WebDriver

Chapter 2 described classes, objects, methods, annotations, access modifiers, and keywords "this and static". A class incorporates data and code that operates on the data. In addition, classes provide a template for objects which is the foundation for object-oriented programming. Methods carry out a specific task while providing access to data defined by the class. Chapter 3 will discuss arrays and strings which are regarded as objects in Java.

Skype: rex.jones34
Twitter: @RexJonesII
Email: Rex.Jones@Test4Success.org
LinkedIn: https://www.linkedin.com/in/rexjones34

Chapter 3
Arrays and Strings

An array is a collection of variables with the same data type, same name and fixed number of values. The values are accessed via an index which identifies an item and starts at zero. Each item in the array is called an element. A benefit of arrays is the capacity to deal with a large number of related values in one entity. For instance, a single array has the ability to hold every employee's salary.

In Java, arrays and strings are considered objects. A string is a data type containing an immutable sequence of characters. Immutable means the string cannot be modified after an initialization statement. However, there are many methods that can perform actions on the strings.

Chapter three will discuss the following concerning arrays and strings:

- ✓ Single-Dimensional Arrays
- ✓ Multi-Dimensional Arrays
- ✓ For-Each Loop
- ✓ Strings

Single-Dimensional Arrays

Single-Dimensional arrays are the most used type of arrays. It stores a list of related values such as daily temperatures for a specific month. In return, the list of values can lead to a monthly temperature average. All of the information stored in an array is easily accessible by an index. The following are two syntaxes for defining a single-dimensional array:

3 Tips To Master Selenium Within 30 Days
http://tinyurl.com/3-Tips-For-Selenium

Free Webinars, Videos, and Live Trainings
http://tinyurl.com/Free-QTP-UFT-Selenium

Chapter 3
Arrays and Strings   (Part 2) Java 4 Selenium WebDriver
Syntax
arrType arrName[] = new arrType[arrSize];

        or

arrType arrName[];
arrName = new arrType[arrSize];

Parameter	Description
arrType	Determines the data type of each value in the array
arrName	Name of the array
new	Allocates memory for the array
arrSize	Number of values in the array

Figure 3.1 – Single Dimension Syntax Details

The following is an example of a single-dimensional array:

Skype: rex.jones34
Twitter: @RexJonesII
Email: Rex.Jones@Test4Success.org
LinkedIn: https://www.linkedin.com/in/rexjones34

Chapter 3
Arrays and Strings   (Part 2) Java 4 Selenium WebDriver

```java
1  public class OneDimensionalArray
2  {
3      public static void main(String[] args)
4      {
5          int [] tempMay = new int [3];
6
7          tempMay[0] = 105;
8          tempMay[1] = 102;
9          tempMay[2] = 98;
10
11         System.out.println("The highest temperature in May was " + tempMay[0] + " degrees");
12         System.out.println("The 2nd highest temperature in May was " + tempMay[1] + " degrees");
13         System.out.println("The 3rd highest temperature in May was " + tempMay[2] + " degrees");
14     }
15 }
```

int [] tempMay = new int [3] initialize the array as having 3 elements "values"

Values are assigned to the array
temp[0] = 105;
temp[1] = 102;
temp[2] = 98;

Figure 3.2 – Single-Dimensional Array Example

Program Output:
```
The highest temperature in May was 105 degrees
The 2nd highest temperature in May was 102 degrees
The 3rd highest temperature in May was 98 degrees
```

- Line 5 initializes the array "tempMay" by using the keyword "new". The number 3 in brackets [3] indicate the array contain 3 elements
- Lines 7 – 9 assign values to each of the array. The first value is stored at index position 0. Zero is always the starting position for arrays. In this example, the last index position is 2. Elements 0 – 2 holds a total of 3 elements.

Arrays can be assigned values on one line without the keyword "new". The following is another way to assign values to an array:

3 Tips To Master Selenium Within 30 Days
http://tinyurl.com/3-Tips-For-Selenium

Free Webinars, Videos, and Live Trainings
http://tinyurl.com/Free-QTP-UFT-Selenium

Chapter 3
Arrays and Strings   (Part 2) Java 4 Selenium WebDriver

```java
 1 public class OneDimensionalArray
 2 {
 3     public static void main(String[] args)
 4     {
 5         int[] tempMay = {105, 102, 98};
 6
 7         System.out.println("The highest temperature in May was " + tempMay[0] + " degrees");
 8         System.out.println("The 2nd highest temperature in May was " + tempMay[1] + " degrees");
 9         System.out.println("The 3rd highest temperature in May was " + tempMay[2] + " degrees");
10     }
11 }
```

The array "**tempMay**" was initialized and assigned values on the same line

Figure 3.3 – Alternate Single-Dimensional Array Example

Program Output:
```
The highest temperature in May was 105 degrees
The 2nd highest temperature in May was 102 degrees
The 3rd highest temperature in May was 98 degrees
```

Line 5 initializes the array "tempMay" and assigns three values to the array. Notice the keyword "new" is not used to initialize the array. However, the data type "int" is specified along with the array name and values. Square brackets indicates an array while the number of values within the curly brackets dictate the array size. The following is a diagram displaying the array values from Figure 3.2 and Figure 3.3:

Skype: rex.jones34
Twitter: @RexJonesII
Email: Rex.Jones@Test4Success.org
LinkedIn: https://www.linkedin.com/in/rexjones34

Chapter 3
Arrays and Strings   (Part 2) Java 4 Selenium WebDriver

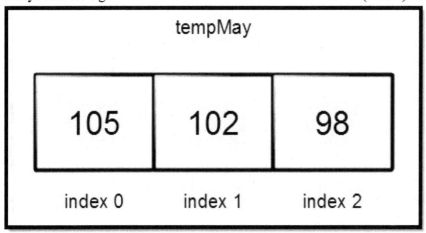

Figure 3.4 – Array Name, Values, and Indexes

Multi-Dimensional Arrays

Multi-Dimensional arrays are regarded as an array of arrays. Therefore two or more brackets
must be used to declare a multi-dimensional array. The most common type of multi-
dimensional array is a two-dimensional array. Each dimension contains its own set of
brackets. A spreadsheet with rows and columns is a good way to imagine a two-dimensional
array. The first pair of brackets are rows and second pair of brackets are columns. The
following is the syntax and example for a two-dimensional array:

Syntax
arrType arrName[] [] – new arrType[arrSize1] [arrSize2];

3 Tips To Master Selenium Within 30 Days
http://tinyurl.com/3-Tips-For-Selenium

Free Webinars, Videos, and Live Trainings
http://tinyurl.com/Free-QTP-UFT-Selenium

Chapter 3
Arrays and Strings   (Part 2) Java 4 Selenium WebDriver

```
1  public class TwoDimensionalArray
2  {
3      public static void main(String[] args)
4      {
5          int row, column;
6
7          int testTwoDimension [][] = new int [2][3];
8
9          for (row = 0; row < 2; row++)
10         {
11             for (column = 0; column < 3; column++)
12             {
13                 testTwoDimension [row][column] = (row*3) + column + 1;
14                 System.out.print(testTwoDimension [row][column] + " ");
15             }
16             System.out.println();
17         }
18     }
19 }
```

> **Two-Dimensional Arrays**
> contains 2 brackets

Figure 3.5 – Two-Dimensional Array Example

Program Output:
```
1 2 3
4 5 6
```

- Line 7 initializes the two-dimensional array "testTwoDimension" by using the keyword "new". Two brackets indicate there are two dimensions similar to rows and columns.
- Notice the output produces a total of two rows and three columns. Line 9 represents the count for rows while line 11 represents the count for column
- Line 13 calculates the values one through six
- Line 14 prints the values one through six

Skype: rex.jones34
Twitter: @RexJonesII
Email: Rex.Jones@Test4Success.org
LinkedIn: https://www.linkedin.com/in/rexjones34

Chapter 3
Arrays and Strings   (Part 2) Java 4 Selenium WebDriver

Comparable to single-dimensional arrays, a two-dimensional array can be declared and initialized without the keyword "new". The following is an example of a two-dimensional array without being initialized using keyword "new".

```java
1  public class TwoDimensionalArray
2  {
3      public static void main(String[] args)
4      {
5          int row, column;
6
7          int testTwoDimension [][] =
8              {
9                  {1, 2, 3},
10                 {4, 5, 6}
11             };
12
13         for (row = 0; row < 2; row++)
14         {
15             for (column = 0; column < 3; column++)
16                 System.out.print(testTwoDimension [row][column] + " ");
17                 System.out.println();
18         }
19     }
20 }
```

The two-dimensional array is declared and initialized with values

Figure 3.6 – Alternate Two-Dimensional Array Example

Program Output:
```
1 2 3
4 5 6
```

Lines 7 – 11 initialize the array by surrounding each dimension's list within a separate set of brackets. Notice how each element is divided by a comma and each set of brackets represent a row. The previous two examples output the same information. A specific value can be printed by indicating a specific row and column. The following example prints a specific value according to a defined row and column:

3 Tips To Master Selenium Within 30 Days
http://tinyurl.com/3-Tips-For-Selenium

Free Webinars, Videos, and Live Trainings
http://tinyurl.com/Free-QTP-UFT-Selenium

Chapter 3
Arrays and Strings

(Part 2) Java 4 Selenium WebDriver

```java
1  public class TwoDimensionalArray
2  {
3      public static void main(String[] args)
4      {
5          int row, column;
6
7          int testTwoDimension [][] =
8              {
9                  {1, 2, 3},
10                 {4, 5, 6}
11             };
12
13         for (row = 0; row < 2; row++)
14         {
15             for (column = 0; column < 3; column++)
16                 System.out.print(testTwoDimension [row][column] + " ");
17                 System.out.println();
18         }
19         System.out.println("\n" + "What value is located in row 1 - column 2? " + testTwoDimension [1][2]);
20     }
21 }
```

This statement prints a specific value from the array

Figure 3.7 – Print A Specific Value From A Two-Dimensional Array

Program Output:
```
1 2 3
4 5 6

What value is located in row 1 - column 2? 6
```

Skype: rex.jones34
Twitter: @RexJonesII
Email: Rex.Jones@Test4Success.org
LinkedIn: https://www.linkedin.com/in/rexjones34

Chapter 3
Arrays and Strings   (Part 2) Java 4 Selenium WebDriver

The following illustrates the output in a spreadsheet format:

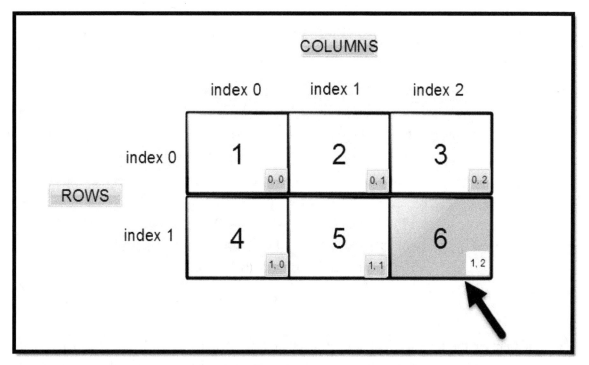

Figure 3.8 – Specific Index For A Two-Dimensional Array

For-Each Loop

The for-each loop (known as enhanced for loop) was established to cycle through a collection of objects such as an array. This type of control structure presents the same functionality as the for loop (see *Chapter 4 - Control Structures in (Part 1) Java 4 Selenium WebDriver*) which executes a block of code a certain number of iterations. However, the for-each loop executes a block of code while cycling through each element in the collection. The following is the for-each loop syntax:

3 Tips To Master Selenium Within 30 Days
http://tinyurl.com/3-Tips-For-Selenium

Free Webinars, Videos, and Live Trainings
http://tinyurl.com/Free-QTP-UFT-Selenium

Chapter 3
Arrays and Strings   (Part 2) Java 4 Selenium WebDriver
Syntax
for (collType itrVariable: collection)
{
  statement(s)
}

Syntax Details

Argument	Description
collType	Refers to the type of data for the collection
itrVariable	Refers to the name of the iteration variable that receives each element after every iteration
collection	The collection such as array that will be iterated or cycled through
statement(s)	The blocked of that will be executed
{ … }	The opening and closing curly brackets

Figure 3.9 – For-Each Loop Syntax Details

All elements in the for-each loop are retrieved and stored in the itrVariable. The loop repeats until all elements are read in index order. It is important to know that the colltype must be the same type as the object. In the case of arrays, the collType must be the same type as the arrType. The following is an example of for-each loop:

Skype: rex.jones34
Twitter: @RexJonesII
Email: Rex.Jones@Test4Success.org
LinkedIn: https://www.linkedin.com/in/rexjones34

Chapter 3
Arrays and Strings   (Part 2) Java 4 Selenium WebDriver

```
1  public class ForEachLoop
2  {
3      public static void main(String[] args)
4      {
5          double[] costPerItem = {12.34, 56.78, 99.99};
6          double totalCost = 0;
7
8          for (double i: costPerItem)
9          {
10             System.out.println("The cost is " + i);
11             totalCost = totalCost + i;
12         }
13         System.out.println("\n" + "The total cost of all items is " + totalCost);
14     }
15 }
```

> The **for-each loop** retrieves each cost per item then calculates the total cost

Figure 3.10 – For Each Loop Example

Program Output:
```
The cost is 12.34
The cost is 56.78
The cost is 99.99

The total cost of all items is 169.11
```

- Line 5 and 6 initialize and assign values to the array "costPerItem" and "totalCost"
- Line 8 retrieves each element (12.34, 56.78, 99.99) in array "costPerItem"
- Line 10 prints each element
- Line 11 calculates the total of all elements

Note: Lines 8 – 11 can be read as "For each double data type in the "costPerItem" array, print each element and calculate the total of all elements".

Two-Dimensional Array Iteration

Iterations for two-dimensional arrays operate similar to single-dimensional arrays. The iteration variable for a two-dimensional array must reference the single-dimensional array. It must reference the single-dimensional array because two-dimensional arrays are considered

3 Tips To Master Selenium Within 30 Days
http://tinyurl.com/3-Tips-For-Selenium

Free Webinars, Videos, and Live Trainings
http://tinyurl.com/Free-QTP-UFT-Selenium

Chapter 3
Arrays and Strings   (Part 2) Java 4 Selenium WebDriver
arrays of arrays. Therefore each two-dimensional array iteration retrieves the next array. The
following is an example of a two-dimensional array iteration:

```
1  public class ForEachLoop
2  {
3      public static void main(String[] args)
4      {
5          int totalCost = 0;
6          int[][] costPerItem =
7              {
8                  {5, 10},
9                  {15, 20},
10                 {25, 30}
11             };
12
13         for (int i[]: costPerItem)
14         {
15             for (int j: i)
16             {
17                 System.out.println("The cost is " + j);
18                 totalCost = totalCost + j;
19             }
20         }
21         System.out.println("\n" + "The total cost of all items is " + totalCost);
22     }
23 }
```

The **for-each loop** retrieves the cost per item in the **two-dimensional array** then calculates the total cost

Figure 3.11 – Two-Dimension Array Iteration Example

Program Output:
```
The cost is 5
The cost is 10
The cost is 15
The cost is 20
The cost is 25
The cost is 30

The total cost of all items is 105
```

- Line 5 initializes and assigns zero "0" to totalCost
- Lines 6 – 11 initialize and assign values to the two-dimensional array "costPerItem"

Skype: rex.jones34
Twitter: @RexJonesII
Email: Rex.Jones@Test4Success.org
LinkedIn: https://www.linkedin.com/in/rexjones34

Chapter 3
Arrays and Strings   (Part 2) Java 4 Selenium WebDriver

- Line 13 "`for (int i[]: costPerItem)`" references a single-dimensional array whereby each iteration retrieves the next array in costPerItem from start to finish "index 0 to index 5"
- Line 15 "`for (int j: i)`" cycles through each element

Search An Array

Arrays can be searched to retrieve specific values. There are times when only a certain value is needed from a collection of values. The following example illustrates how to retrieve a specific value from an array:

```
1  public class ForEachLoop
2  {
3      public static void main(String[] args)
4      {
5          int specificCost = 20;
6          int[][] costPerItem =
7              {
8                  {5, 10},
9                  {15, 20},
10                 {25, 30}
11             };
12
13         for (int i[]: costPerItem)
14         {
15             for (int j: i)
16             {
17                 if (j == specificCost)
18                 {
19                     System.out.println("The specific cost of " + "'" + specificCost + "'" + " was located in the collection of values");
20                 }
21             }
22         }
23     }
24 }
```

The **if branch** searches the two-dimensional array for a **specific value**

Figure 3.12 – Search A Two-Dimensional Array

Program Output:
The specific cost of '20' was located in the collection of values

3 Tips To Master Selenium Within 30 Days
http://tinyurl.com/3-Tips-For-Selenium

Free Webinars, Videos, and Live Trainings
http://tinyurl.com/Free-QTP-UFT-Selenium

Chapter 3
Arrays and Strings   (Part 2) Java 4 Selenium WebDriver

- Line 5 initializes and assigns 20 to variable "specificCost"
- Lines 6 – 11 initialize and assign values to the two-dimensional array "costPerItem"
- Line 13 "`for (int i[]: costPerItem)`" references a single-dimensional array whereby each iteration retrieves the next array in costPerItem from start to finish "index 0 to index 5"
- Line 15 "`for (int j: i)`" cycles through each element
- Line 17 searches the two-dimensional array for a specific element "20" via variable specificCost

Strings

A string is a data type containing an immutable sequence of characters. This data type is considered an object so it was not discussed in *(Part 1) Java 4 Selenium WebDriver* with the other data types. There are two ways to create a string:

1. String Literal
2. String using the keyword "new"

The following is an example of a string literal:

Chapter 3
Arrays and Strings
(Part 2) Java 4 Selenium WebDriver

```java
1 public class StringObject
2 {
3    public static void main(String[] args)
4    {
5        String firstName = "Rex";
6        String lastName = "Jones";
7
8        System.out.println("Strings are placed within quotation marks");
9        System.out.print("The first name is " + firstName + " and last name is " + lastName + ".");
10       System.out.println(" Both names were declared and initialized as strings. A sequence of characters");
11   }
12 }
```

The highlighted text are strings

Figure 3.13 – String Example

Program Output:
```
Strings are placed within quotation marks
The first name is Rex and last name is Jones. Both names were declared and
initialized as strings. A sequence of characters
```

- Lines 5 and 6 declare and initialize a string data type
- Lines 8 – 10 displays the string literal within the println method ()

Strings can be created like other objects by using the keyword "new" which calls the String constructor. The following is an example of a String with the keyword "new":

String name = **new** String ("Rex Jones");

String Operations
In Java, there is a String class which contains many methods for operations. The following is a screenshot of several String methods per Eclipse:

3 Tips To Master Selenium Within 30 Days
http://tinyurl.com/3-Tips-For-Selenium

Free Webinars, Videos, and Live Trainings
http://tinyurl.com/Free-QTP-UFT-Selenium

Chapter 3
Arrays and Strings   (Part 2) Java 4 Selenium WebDriver

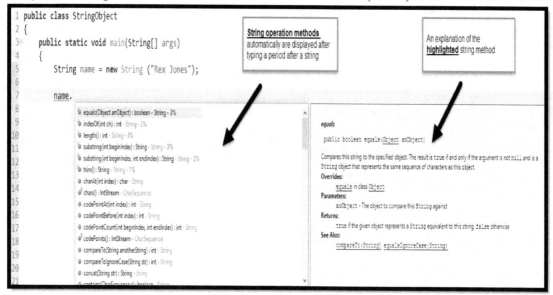

Figure 3.14 – String Methods

- Line 7 displays a list of methods after typing a period after the variable "name"
- A description of a specific method "equals" appears when it is highlighted

The following are popular **String methods**, their data type, and description:

1. **charAt (int index)**: char - Returns the character at the specified index
2. **compareTo (str)**: int - Returns less than zero if the calling string is less than str, greater than zero if the calling string is greater than str, and zero if the strings are equal
3. **concat (String str)**: String - Concatenates the given string at the end of the string
4. **equals (Object anObject)**: boolean – Compares the string to a specific object
5. **equalsIgnoreCase (String string)**: boolean - Compare strings and ignore the cases

Skype: rex.jones34
Twitter: @RexJonesII
Email: Rex.Jones@Test4Success.org
LinkedIn: https://www.linkedin.com/in/rexjones34

Chapter 3

Arrays and Strings   (Part 2) Java 4 Selenium WebDriver

6. **indexOf (String str)**: int - Returns the index of the first occurrence of a specified substring

7. **lastindexOf (String str)**: int - Returns the index of the last occurrence of a string

8. **length ()**: int - Returns the length of a string

9. **replace (char oldChar, char newChar)**: String - Returns the new string after changing all occurrences of the old string

10. **split (String regex)**: String[] - Splits the string and returns a string array that matches the given regular expression

11. **toLowerCase ()**: String - Converts all of the characters in a String to lower case

12. **toUpperCase ()**: String - Converts all of the characters in a String to upper case

13. **trim ()**: String - Returns a copy of the string, after deleting leading and trailing white spaces from the original string

A string data type cannot be combined with a different data type for an operation such as multiplication, subtraction, or division. For example, a string value of "534000.00" appears to be a numeric value but string does not allow mathematical operations unless a type wrapper converts the string. The value "534000.00" resembles a double data type. However, an error occurs if combined with a double data type. The following example displays an error if a string data type is combined with a subtraction operator:

```
 1  public class StringObject
 2  {
 3      public static void main(String[] args)
 4      {
 5          String grossIncome = "534000.00";
 6          double gross = 534000.00;
 7          double taxes = 225000.00;
 8          double netIncome;
 9
10          netIncome = grossIncome - taxes;
11          netIncome = gross - taxes;
12
13          System.out.println("The net income is " + netIncome);
14      }
15  }
```

> An error occurs because strings does not allow **mathematical operations** although the value "**534000.00**" appears to be numeric.

Figure 3.15 – String Error Due To Mathematical Operations

- Line 5 declares and initializes a Sting value "534000.00"
- Line 10 displays an error because Strings do not allow mathematical operations. However, notice line 11 does not display an error because both variables "gross and taxes" are declared as a double data type "lines 6 and 7"

Type Wrappers

Type wrappers are used to convert strings into primitive types (byte, double, float, integer, long, short). Therefore the previous example which displayed an error for string value "534000.00" can be converted into a number. Type wrappers are used to wrap the primitive type. The following is an example of how to return a double when the value "534000" is specified as a string:

Skype: rex.jones34
Twitter: @RexJonesII
Email: Rex.Jones@Test4Success.org
LinkedIn: https://www.linkedin.com/in/rexjones34

Chapter 3
Arrays and Strings   (Part 2) Java 4 Selenium WebDriver

```java
 1  public class StringObject
 2  {
 3      public static void main(String[] args)
 4      {
 5          String grossIncome = "534000.00";
 6          double taxes = 225000.00;
 7          double netIncome;
 8
 9          netIncome = Double.parseDouble(grossIncome) - taxes;
10
11          System.out.println("The net income is " + netIncome);
12      }
13  }
```

> **Double.*parseDouble*** reads the string value "**grossIncome**" then returns a double data type

Figure 3.16 – Returns A Double After Reading A String Value

Program Output:
```
The net income is 309000.00
```

- Line 5 declares and initializes a Sting value "534000.00"
- Line 9 parses (known as reads) the string "grossIncome" then return a double data type. Afterwards, the variable taxes "225000" is subtracted from variable grossIncome "534000" and the value is assigned to variable "netIncome"

The following is a list of type wrappers that convert a string data type:

Wrapper	Conversion Method
Double	Double.parseDouble(string)
Float	Float.parseFloat(string)
Long	Long.parseLong(string)
Integer	Integer.parseInteger(string)

3 Tips To Master Selenium Within 30 Days
http://tinyurl.com/3-Tips-For-Selenium

Free Webinars, Videos, and Live Trainings
http://tinyurl.com/Free-QTP-UFT-Selenium

Short	String.parseString(string)
Byte	Byte.parseByte(string)

Figure 3.17 – Type Wrappers

Chapter 3 explained arrays and strings which are objects. An array is a collection of variables with the same data type, same name and fixed number of values. A string is a data type containing an immutable sequence of characters. Chapter 4 will discuss the three concepts of Object-Oriented Programming (OOP): inheritance, encapsulation, and polymorphism.

Skype: rex.jones34
Twitter: @RexJonesII
Email: Rex.Jones@Test4Success.org
LinkedIn: https://www.linkedin.com/in/rexjones34

Chapter 4
Object-Oriented Programming (OOP)

Object-Oriented Programming (OOP) is the heart of Java programming. As a result, there is no way to separate OOP from Java. An understanding of OOP is important for Java programming. OOP consist of the following three concepts: inheritance, encapsulation, and polymorphism.

Inheritance is a hierarchical concept that extends reusable code and objects. A superclass is created with variables and methods then inherited by other classes. The inherited classes are called subclasses. All subclasses inherit superclass members and permitted to add their own class members. For example, a dog is an animal, so the class "Dog", would be a subclass of Animal. A cat is an animal and the class "Cat" would be a subclass of Animal. In both examples, class "Animal" is the superclass while "Dog and Cat" are subclasses.

Encapsulation is a programming concept that combines data and code via a class. Classes are like containers that protect / hide class members via access modifiers. Protection is important for managing data. Access modifiers and accessor methods provide a way to set and return data.

Polymorphism is a concept that allows multiple methods to use one interface. One method contains a structure implemented by many methods. A given class specifies the method and allows other classes to define a specific implementation for that method.

Chapter four will explain the following regarding Object-Oriented Programming (OOP):

- ✓ Inheritance
- ✓ Encapsulation
- ✓ Polymorphism

3 Tips To Master Selenium Within 30 Days
http://tinyurl.com/3-Tips-For-Selenium

Free Webinars, Videos, and Live Trainings
http://tinyurl.com/Free-QTP-UFT-Selenium

Chapter 4
Object-Oriented Programming (OOP)   (Part 2) Java 4 Selenium WebDriver

Inheritance

The concept of inheriting classes is an important foundation within object-oriented programming. Functionalities are added to an existing class which prevents the same code from being written multiple times. The subclass inherits all class members from the superclass. Another way to view superclass and subclass, is to think of superclass as the parent and subclass as the child.

In order for the subclass to inherit the superclass, the keyword "extends" must be used in the class declaration. Keyword "extends" means the subclass will add to the superclass. Subclasses are not allowed to inherit multiple superclasses. However, a subclass is allowed to become a superclass for an additional subclass. As a result, the additional subclass inherits all class members from each superclass. The following is the syntax for a subclass inheriting a superclass:

Syntax
class SubClassName **extends** SuperClassName
{
        //Class Body
}

The following is an example for a subclass inheriting a superclass:

Skype: rex.jones34
Twitter: @RexJonesII
Email: Rex.Jones@Test4Success.org
LinkedIn: https://www.linkedin.com/in/rexjones34

Chapter 4
Object-Oriented Programming (OOP)   (Part 2) Java 4 Selenium WebDriver

```
 1  class School
 2  {
 3      int numTeachers;
 4      int numStudents;
 5
 6      void showNumberOfPeople ()
 7      {
 8          System.out.println("There are " + numTeachers + " teachers and " + numStudents + " students");
 9      }
10  }
11  class ElementarySchool extends School
12  {
13      String principalName;
14
15      int totalTeacherStudents ()
16      {
17          return numTeachers + numStudents;
18      }
19
20      void displayPrincipal ()
21      {
22          System.out.println("The principal name is " + principalName);
23      }
24  }
25  class SchoolDistrict
26  {
27      public static void main(String[] args)
28      {
29          ElementarySchool BishopHeights = new ElementarySchool ();
30          ElementarySchool AltaMesa = new ElementarySchool ();
31
32          BishopHeights.numTeachers = 10;
33          BishopHeights.numStudents = 130;
34          BishopHeights.principalName = "Joe Doe";
35
36          System.out.println("My elementary school is Bishop Heights \n");
37          BishopHeights.displayPrincipal ();
38          BishopHeights.showNumberOfPeople ();
39          System.out.println("Therefore the total of teachers and students is " + BishopHeights.totalTeacherStudents () );
40      }
41  }
```

> The class "**ElementarySchool**" is a subclass while "**School**" is a superclass.

Figure 4.1 – Subclass Extends Superclass Example

Program Output:
```
My elementary school is Bishop Heights

The principal name is Joe Doe
There are 10 teachers and 130 students
Therefore the total of teachers and students is 140
```

- Line 1 displays superclass "School"
- Line 11 uses the keyword "extends" to create subclass "ElementarySchool" which inherits superclass "School"
- Line 17 utilize variables "numTeachers and numStudents" of the superclass
- Lines 29 and 30 display two objects "BishopHeights and AltaMesa"

3 Tips To Master Selenium Within 30 Days
http://tinyurl.com/3-Tips-For-Selenium

Free Webinars, Videos, and Live Trainings
http://tinyurl.com/Free-QTP-UFT-Selenium

Chapter 4
Object-Oriented Programming (OOP)   (Part 2) Java 4 Selenium WebDriver

- Lines 32 and 33 assign values "10 and 130" to variables "numTeachers and numStudents" which are inherited from superclass "School"
- Line 34 assign a value "Joe Doe" to variable "principalName" which is a member of subclass "Elementary School"

The subclass "ElementarySchool" is a unique type of superclass "School". More subclasses such as HighSchool, University, etc. can inherit superclass "School". The "ElementarySchool" class inherits all of the "School" class members then add a variable "principalName" and two methods "totalTeacherStudents and displayPrincipal". Notice how line 30 creates an object that was not utilized. This shows that more Elementary School objects can be created to access members of the superclass "School".

Note: Objects from the superclass do not have knowledge of the subclass. Therefore, the superclass objects cannot access the subclass.

Superclass Object

The superclass "Object" is the highest superclass of all classes. In other words, there is no parent class above the "Object" superclass. By default, the "Object" superclass includes methods that are inherited by all subclasses. The following is a screenshot which shows Object "java.lang.Object" by default as the Superclass when creating a new class:

Skype: rex.jones34
Twitter: @RexJonesII
Email: Rex.Jones@Test4Success.org
LinkedIn: https://www.linkedin.com/in/rexjones34

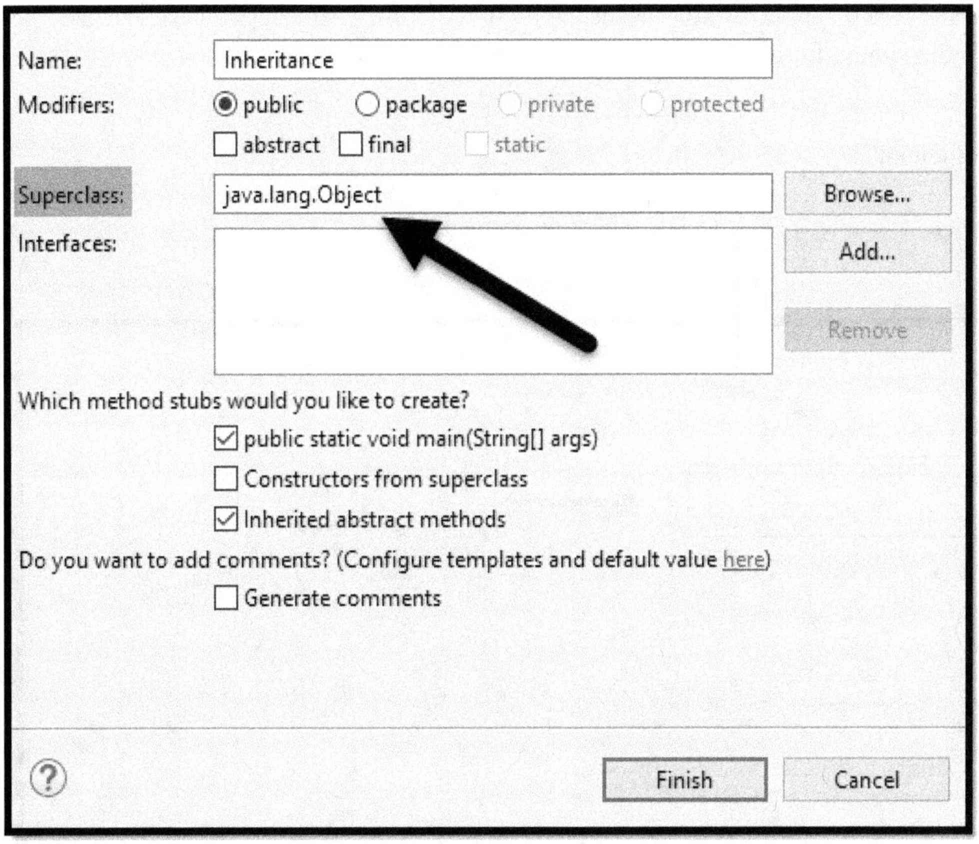

Chapter 4
Object-Oriented Programming (OOP)   (Part 2) Java 4 Selenium WebDriver

Figure 4.2 – Eclipse New Class Creation Modal

Superclass and Subclass Constructors

Superclasses and subclasses contain their own constructors, which initialize objects of its class. As a result, the constructors are independent of each other. The superclass does not have access to the subclass constructors but the subclass has access to the superclass constructors. Subclasses call a superclass's constructor by utilizing the keyword "super". In

3 Tips To Master Selenium Within 30 Days
http://tinyurl.com/3-Tips-For-Selenium

Free Webinars, Videos, and Live Trainings
http://tinyurl.com/Free-QTP-UFT-Selenium

Chapter 4
Object-Oriented Programming (OOP)   (Part 2) Java 4 Selenium WebDriver
addition, the keyword "super" allows access to hidden members of a superclass. The
following is the syntax for a subclass calling a superclass constructor:

Syntax
super (parameter-list)

The following is an example of a subclass inheriting a superclass:

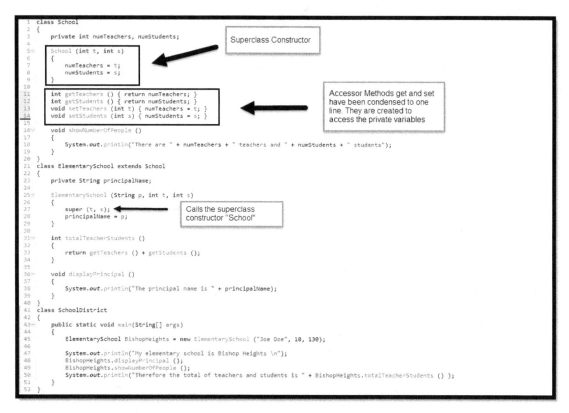

Figure 4.3 – Subclass Inherits Superclass Example

Skype: rex.jones34
Twitter: @RexJonesII
Email: Rex.Jones@Test4Success.org
LinkedIn: https://www.linkedin.com/in/rexjones34

Chapter 4
Object-Oriented Programming (OOP)   (Part 2) Java 4 Selenium WebDriver

Program Output:

```
My elementary school is Bishop Heights

The principal name is Joe Doe
There are 10 teachers and 130 students
Therefore the total of teachers and students is 140
```

- Line 3 declares all of the variables "numTeachers and numStudents" as private
- Lines 5 – 9 is the constructor for superclass "School"
- Lines 11 – 14 are the accessor methods "get and set"
- Lines 25 – 29 is the subclass constructor for "ElementarySchool" which calls the superclass constructor "School". The statement "**super** (t, s);" on line 27 refers to the superclass constructor via keyword "super"

Note: A superclass constructor is executed first if the program includes a superclass constructor and subclass constructor.

Abstraction

Abstraction applies to classes as well as methods. The keyword "abstract" is used to create abstract classes and methods. An abstract class cannot be instantiated so it is used as a superclass. Abstract methods are declared without an implementation so it does not include a body. Abstract classes can include abstract methods and implemented methods. However, an abstract class cannot contain objects due to incomplete implementation of its methods.

The purpose of abstract classes is to only define a generalized method then allow a subclass to define the details of the method. There are situations when a superclass cannot create a meaningful method implementation. An instance method can be declared abstract but static methods and constructors cannot be declared abstract. The following is the syntax for an abstract class and method:

Syntax – Abstract Class

3 Tips To Master Selenium Within 30 Days
http://tinyurl.com/3-Tips-For-Selenium

Free Webinars, Videos, and Live Trainings
http://tinyurl.com/Free-QTP-UFT-Selenium

Chapter 4
Object-Oriented Programming (OOP)   (Part 2) Java 4 Selenium WebDriver

abstract class ClassName
{
　　　// Abstract Classes can contain abstract methods and implemented methods

　　　// Abstract Method
　　　abstract methodType methodName (parameter-list);

　　　// Implemented Method
　　　methodType methodName (parameter-list)
　　　{
　　　　　// Method Body
　　　}
}

Syntax – Abstract Method
abstract methodType methodName (parameter-list);

Note: A subclass must be declared as abstract or implement all of the abstract methods from the superclass.

Encapsulation

The concept of encapsulation consists of binding code and data. A class encapsulates code and data giving structure to the class members. As a result of this structure, the code has access to manipulate data while preventing interference from outside sources.

Declaring a variable as private is one of the ways to prevent interference. Private is an access modifier that only allow a class member (variable or method) to be accessed within its own class. However, the accessor methods provide a bridge to private variables. Although there is a bridge, each private variable remains safe from misuse such as entering a negative value for only positive values.

Skype: rex.jones34
Twitter: @RexJonesII
Email: Rex.Jones@Test4Success.org
LinkedIn: https://www.linkedin.com/in/rexjones34

Chapter 4
Object-Oriented Programming (OOP)   (Part 2) Java 4 Selenium WebDriver
Access Modifiers

Access modifiers are helpful features of object-oriented programming. They are helpful because of the access limitation it places on every class and class members (variables and methods). In Java, there are four kinds of access modifiers:

1. public – indicates a member can be accessed by all classes
2. protected – indicates a member can be accessed by all classes and subclasses within its own package (*see Packages in Chapter 5*)
3. no modifier – indicates a member can be accessed by all classes within its own package
4. private – indicates a member can be accessed within its own class

The access modifier precedes a class, variable, and method declaration. Classes can only use the public modifier or no modifier. Therefore, an error occurs if a class makes use of a private or protected access modifier. The following is an example of a class, method, and variables using a public modifier:

3 Tips To Master Selenium Within 30 Days
http://tinyurl.com/3-Tips-For-Selenium

Free Webinars, Videos, and Live Trainings
http://tinyurl.com/Free-QTP-UFT-Selenium

Chapter 4
Object-Oriented Programming (OOP)   (Part 2) Java 4 Selenium WebDriver

```
1  public class English
2  {
3      public int students, weeks, days;
4
5      public int totalDays ()
6      {
7          return weeks * days;
8      }
9  }
10
11 class TwoEnglishCourses
12 {
13     public static void main (String args[])
14     {
15         English ENG101 = new English ();
16         English ENG202 = new English ();
17
18         ENG101.students = 10;
19         ENG101.weeks = 4;
20         ENG101.days = 3;
21
22         ENG202.students = 12;
23         ENG202.weeks = 6;
24         ENG202.days = 3;
25
26         System.out.println("The English 101 course has " + ENG101.students + " students and the course last " + ENG101.totalDays () + " days");
27         System.out.println("The English 202 course has " + ENG202.students + " students and the course last " + ENG202.totalDays () + " days");
28     }
29 }
```

> The **class** "English" is declared **public**
> The **variables** "students, weeks, days" are declared **public**
> The **method** "totalDays ()" is declared **public**

Figure 4.4 – Public Class, Variables, and Method

The class (line 1), all of the variables (line 3), and method (lines 5 - 8) are declared with a public access modifier. Consequently, there are no errors and the members within the English class can be accessed by code from the class "TwoEnglishCourses".

The following is an example of a private method:

Skype: rex.jones34
Twitter: @RexJonesII
Email: Rex.Jones@Test4Success.org
LinkedIn: https://www.linkedin.com/in/rexjones34

Chapter 4
Object-Oriented Programming (OOP)   (Part 2) Java 4 Selenium WebDriver

```
1  public class English
2  {
3     public int students, weeks, days;
4
5=    private int totalDays ()        ◄——    The method totalDays () is
6     {                                       declared private
7       return weeks * days;
8     }
9  }
10
11 class TwoEnglishCourses
12 {
13=   public static void main (String args[])
14    {
15      English ENG101 = new English ();
16      English ENG202 = new English ();
17
18      ENG101.students = 10;
19      ENG101.weeks = 4;
20      ENG101.days = 3;
21
22      ENG202.students = 12;
23      ENG202.weeks = 6;
24      ENG202.days = 3;
25
26      System.out.println("The English 101 course has " + ENG101.students + " students and the course last " + ENG101.totalDays () + " days");
27      [The method totalDays() from the type English is not visible] 202 course has " + ENG202.students + " students and the course last " + ENG202.totalDays () + " days");
28    }
29 }
```

The calls to method totalDays () from
ENG101.totalDays () and
ENG202.totalDays () cause an error

Figure 4.5 – Private Method

Line 5 declares the method totalDays () with a private access modifier. That means only members within its class "English" can access the method. Lines 26 and 27 attempts to call method "totalDays ()" but cannot because they are located in a different class "TwoEnglishCourses". As a result, an error message states "The method totalDays ()" from Type English is not visible. The following is an example of one private variable and two public variables:

3 Tips To Master Selenium Within 30 Days
http://tinyurl.com/3-Tips-For-Selenium

Free Webinars, Videos, and Live Trainings
http://tinyurl.com/Free-QTP-UFT-Selenium

Chapter 4
Object-Oriented Programming (OOP)   (Part 2) Java 4 Selenium WebDriver

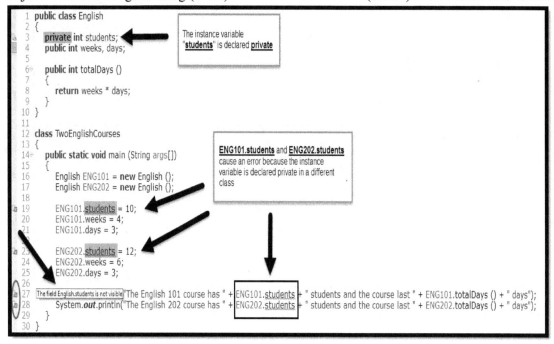

Figure 4.6 – Private and Public Instance Variables

Line 3 declares instance variable "students" as private while line 4 declares instance
variables "weeks and days" as public. Notice lines 19 – 25, two errors "lines 19 and 23"
occur for the private variable "students". In addition, there is an error on lines 27 and 28
which states "The field English.students is not visible". The private variable is only visible to
the English class but not visible to the class "TwoEnglishCourses". However, the public
variables are visible to both classes. The following are access levels for each modifier:

Chapter 4
Object-Oriented Programming (OOP)   (Part 2) Java 4 Selenium WebDriver

	public	protected	no modifier	private
Class	Yes	Yes	Yes	Yes
Package	Yes	Yes	Yes	No
Subclass	Yes	Yes	No	No
World	Yes	No	No	No

Figure 4.7 – Access Modifier Levels

Accessor Methods (Getter & Setter Methods)

Access methods are known as getter and setter methods. The methods are implemented to get and set values of private variables. Private variables can only be accessed by code within its own class. Therefore the accessor methods are two methods in the same class as the private variables.

Both methods are defined with a prefix that begins with "get" and "set" before the method name. For example, getDays () and setDays () are regarded as accessor methods to get the number of days then set the number of days. Setter methods protect data from misuse while getter methods return data to the outside source. The following is an example of both accessor methods:

3 Tips To Master Selenium Within 30 Days
http://tinyurl.com/3-Tips-For-Selenium

Free Webinars, Videos, and Live Trainings
http://tinyurl.com/Free-QTP-UFT-Selenium

Chapter 4
Object-Oriented Programming (OOP)   (Part 2) Java 4 Selenium WebDriver

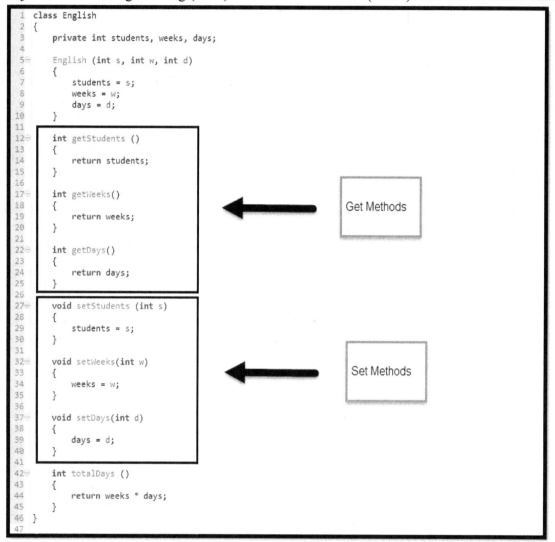

Figure 4.8 – Accessor Methods

- Line 3 declares all of the instance variables "students, weeks, and days" as <u>private</u>

Skype: rex.jones34
Twitter: @RexJonesII
Email: Rex.Jones@Test4Success.org
LinkedIn: https://www.linkedin.com/in/rexjones34

Chapter 4
Object-Oriented Programming (OOP)   (Part 2) Java 4 Selenium WebDriver

- Lines 5 – 10 is the constructor method
- Lines 12 – 25 are the get accessor methods. Each method only get/return the number of students, weeks, and days
- Lines 27 – 40 are the set access methods. Each method sets/modifies the number students, weeks, and days

Inheriting Private Members

Private members that are inherited from the superclass remain private in the subclass. Therefore the subclass cannot access the private members. Variables and methods are only accessible by code within its own class which does not include subclasses. Nevertheless, the private members can be accessed by using accessor methods.

Polymorphism

Polymorphism is a significant concept in object-oriented programming. This concept allows one interface to be utilized by multiple methods. In the case of superclass and subclass, a superclass provides a structure whereby a subclass can define its own method operation. The methods are inherited automatically when the subclass extends the superclass.

Method Overriding vs Method Overloading

Method overriding is a feature when the subclass method overrides the superclass method. Both methods must have the same method data type and signature. A method's signature consists of a method's name and parameter list. The superclass method can be called although it is overridden by a subclass method. It is overridden if the keyword "super" and dot (.) operator is followed by the method name: **super**.methodName();

Method overloading is two or more methods in the same class with the same name but a different parameter list. The parameter list determines which overloaded method is executed if a call is made to the method name. However a duplicate method error occurs if multiple methods have the same signature. The following shows the differences between method overriding and method overloading:

3 Tips To Master Selenium Within 30 Days
http://tinyurl.com/3-Tips-For-Selenium

Free Webinars, Videos, and Live Trainings
http://tinyurl.com/Free-QTP-UFT-Selenium

Chapter 4
Object-Oriented Programming (OOP)   (Part 2) Java 4 Selenium WebDriver

	Method Overriding	Method Overloading
Definition	The superclass and subclass has a method with the same method type and signature	A class has multiple methods with the same name and different parameter list
Method Type	The superclass and subclass method types must be compatible	The type can be the same or different
Signature	The superclass and subclass must have the same signature	The signatures are different regarding number of parameters, type of parameters, and order of parameters

Figure 4.9 – Differences Between Method Overriding and Overloading

Note: An "@Override" annotation can be used to instruct the compiler of a subclass overriding a superclass. Annotations make the program easier to read and lets the compiler verify if the override is valid.

Static Binding

Binding is the connection between a method call and the method definition. Static binding (known as early binding) is when binding occurs at compile time. Therefore binding happens before a program executes. The following is an example of static binding:

Skype: rex.jones34
Twitter: @RexJonesII
Email: Rex.Jones@Test4Success.org
LinkedIn: https://www.linkedin.com/in/rexjones34

Chapter 4
Object-Oriented Programming (OOP)   (Part 2) Java 4 Selenium WebDriver

```java
 1  class Binding
 2  {
 3      void printClassName()
 4      {
 5          System.out.println("This class is called Binding");
 6      }
 7  }
 8
 9  class BindingExtend extends Binding
10  {
11      @Override
12      void printClassName()
13      {
14          System.out.println("This class is called BindingExtend");
15      }
16  }
17
18  class BindingExamples
19  {
20      public static void main(String[] args)
21      {
22          BindingExtend objBindingExtend = new BindingExtend ();
23          objBindingExtend.printClassName();
24      }
25  }
```

Static Binding

Figure 4.10 – Static Binding Example

Program Output:
This class is called BindingExtend

- Line 11 displays an annotation which indicates the subclass method "printClassName()" will override the superclass method "printClassName()"
- Line 12 displays an icon next to the line number which has a tooltip that states "overrides Binding.printClassName"
- Line 22 creates an object "objBindingExtend" of class "BindingExtend"
- Line 23 calls the method definition "printClassName()"

Note: For static binding, the compiler verifies if a method definition "printClassName" exist in class "BindingExtend".

3 Tips To Master Selenium Within 30 Days
http://tinyurl.com/3-Tips-For-Selenium

Free Webinars, Videos, and Live Trainings
http://tinyurl.com/Free-QTP-UFT-Selenium

Chapter 4
Object-Oriented Programming (OOP)   (Part 2) Java 4 Selenium WebDriver

Dynamic Binding

Dynamic binding is when binding occurs at run time. Therefore this type of binding happens when the program is running. Unlike static binding, dynamic binding allows polymorphism. Therefore a method override is good illustration of dynamic binding. The following is an example of dynamic binding:

```java
1  class Binding
2  {
3      void printClassName()
4      {
5          System.out.println("This class is called Binding");
6      }
7  }
8
9  class BindingExtend extends Binding
10 {
11     @Override
12     void printClassName()
13     {
14         System.out.println("This class is called BindingExtend");
15     }
16 }
17
18 class BindingExamples
19 {
20     public static void main(String[] args)
21     {
22         Binding objBinding = new Binding ();
23         objBinding.printClassName();          <-- Dynamic Binding
24
25         Binding objBindingExtend = new BindingExtend ();
26         objBindingExtend.printClassName();    <--
27     }
28 }
```

Figure 4.11 – Dynamic Binding Example

Program Output:
```
This class is called Binding
This class is called BindingExtend
```

Skype: rex.jones34
Twitter: @RexJonesII
Email: Rex.Jones@Test4Success.org
LinkedIn: https://www.linkedin.com/in/rexjones34

Chapter 4
Object-Oriented Programming (OOP)   (Part 2) Java 4 Selenium WebDriver

- Lines 3 and 12 define the same method name "printClassName()" for each class "Binding and BindingExtend"
- Lines 22 and 25 creates both objects "objBinding" and "objBindingExtend"
- Lines 23 and 26 is where dynamic binding takes place. Both calls are made to the same method name "printClassName()" but in different classes "superclass and subclass". The objects "objBinding" and "objBindingExtend" are used for binding at run time.

Keyword Final

The keyword "final" prevents a class or method from being overwritten. Methods are implicitly declared as final if the class is declared final. Recall from *Part 1 – Java 4 Selenium WebDriver*, the keyword "final" is used to declare and initialize constants. Constants are unchangeable values assigned to a variable name. The benefit of using keyword "final" is to confirm a class or class member will not change because it is critical to the program. As a result, an error occurs if there is an attempt to inherit a class or override a class member (method or variable) declared as final.

Chapter 4 explained inheritance, encapsulation, and polymorphism. Inheritance is a hierarchical concept which allows reusable code and objects to be extended. Encapsulation protects data by using access modifiers and accessor methods. Polymorphism allows multiple methods to utilize one interface. Chapter 5 will dive into packages which is a group of related classes.

3 Tips To Master Selenium Within 30 Days
http://tinyurl.com/3-Tips-For-Selenium

Free Webinars, Videos, and Live Trainings
http://tinyurl.com/Free-QTP-UFT-Selenium

Chapter 5
Packages

A package is a collection of related classes whereby the package operates like a folder to organize code. The classes within a package are accessed by the package name. Recall from *Part 1 – Java 4 Selenium WebDriver*, that an error occurs if a class makes use of the private access modifier. However, a class can be made private and not accessed by code outside of the package by using no modifier. A package defines a unique namespace which prevents multiple classes of having the same name within a package. In Java, there is no problem with different packages using the same class name.

Chapter 5 will explain the following regarding packages:

- ✓ Create A Package
- ✓ Import A Package
- ✓ Java Class Library

Create A Package

A programmer can create their own package to group classes. All classes have a package that is stored in a directory. The first line in most source files includes a package statement. However, a package statement is optional so the first line can remain blank. A blank package statement is the default which contains no name. It is important to know that different source files are allowed to use the same package statement. The following is the syntax for a package statement:

Syntax
package packagename;

Skype: rex.jones34
Twitter: @RexJonesII
Email: Rex.Jones@Test4Success.org
LinkedIn: https://www.linkedin.com/in/rexjones34

Chapter 5
Packages   (Part 2) Java 4 Selenium WebDriver

The name of each package "e.g., packagename" is case sensitive. In Java, it is conventional
to use all lowercase letters for a package name. All lowercase letters for a package serves as a
clear distinction from class names, method names and most variable names. Eclipse IDE
displays a warning if the first letter within package name begins with a capital letter. The
following is a screenshot which shows a warning if the first letter is a capital letter:

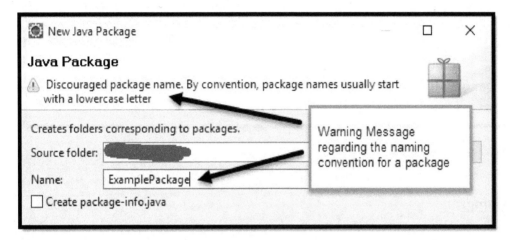

Figure 5.1 – Package Naming Convention

The following is an example of a package statement:

3 Tips To Master Selenium Within 30 Days
http://tinyurl.com/3-Tips-For-Selenium

Free Webinars, Videos, and Live Trainings
http://tinyurl.com/Free-QTP-UFT-Selenium

Chapter 5
Packages   (Part 2) Java 4 Selenium WebDriver

```
 1  package examplepackage;
 2
 3  class PackageTest
 4  {
 5      void printTest ()
 6      {
 7          System.out.println("This is a test");
 8      }
 9  }
10
11  public class Package
12  {
13      public static void main (String args[])
14      {
15          System.out.println("This is another test");
16      }
17  }
```

The package statement
"package examplepackage;"
is located on the first line

Class Names "**PackageTest
and Package**" are components
of package "**examplepackage**"

Figure 5.2 – Package Statement

Program Output:
This is another test

- Line 1 contains the package statement "package examplepackage"
- Line 3 begins the class definition for class "PackageTest". This class is a component of a package "examplepackage"
- Line 11 begins the class definition for class "Package". This class is a component of a package "examplepackage"

The following is a screenshot of the classes grouped together in a package directory:

Skype: rex.jones34
Twitter: @RexJonesII
Email: Rex.Jones@Test4Success.org
LinkedIn: https://www.linkedin.com/in/rexjones34

Chapter 5
Packages   (Part 2) Java 4 Selenium WebDriver

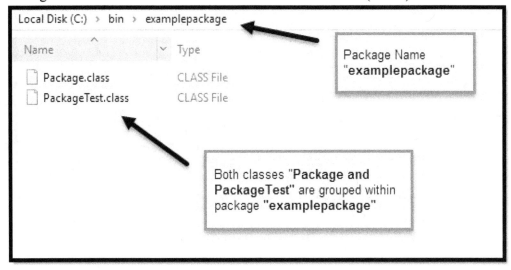

Figure 5.3 – Package Directory Screenshot

Import A Package

A Java package is imported by using the keyword "import". Imports are useful when a class wants to access a member in another class. The other class can be in the same package or different package. After importing a package, the members of the package are used directly without any additional syntax. The following is the syntax for importing a package:

Syntax
import packagename.ClassName;

To import a class, the dot (.) operator is placed between the package name and class name. The import statements must be entered after the package statement but before the classes are declared in the current file. The following is an example of a package statement, import statement, and a class declaration:

3 Tips To Master Selenium Within 30 Days
http://tinyurl.com/3-Tips-For-Selenium

Free Webinars, Videos, and Live Trainings
http://tinyurl.com/Free-QTP-UFT-Selenium

Chapter 5
Packages   (Part 2) Java 4 Selenium WebDriver

```
1  package examplepackage;
2  import examplepackage.PackageTest;        ◀──────        Class "PackageTest"
3                                                            was imported from the
4  public class PackageOne                                  same package
5  {                                                        "examplepackage"
6      public static void main (String args[])
7      {
8          PackageTest objPackage = new PackageTest ();  ◀──    The type "PackageTest" was
9                                                                used to create an object
10         objPackage.printTest();                              "objPackage" after importing
11     }                                                        the class "PackageTest"
12 }
```

Figure 5.4 – Package Import

Program Output:
This is a test

- Line 1 contains the package statement "**package** examplepackage;"
- Line 2 contains the import statement "**import** examplepackage.PackageTest;". The package name is "examplepackage" and class name is "PackageTest" which is located in a different file.
- Line 4 begins the class declaration "**public class** PackageOne"
- Line 8 creates an object "objPackage" using the imported class "PackageTest"
- Line 10 calls the method "printTest();" which is located in class "PackageTest". View Figure 5.2 - Package Statement, to see details of the method.

Note: All of the classes from a specific package can be imported by using the package name and an asterisk: **import** packagename.*;

Skype: rex.jones34
Twitter: @RexJonesII
Email: Rex.Jones@Test4Success.org
LinkedIn: https://www.linkedin.com/in/rexjones34

Chapter 5
Packages   (Part 2) Java 4 Selenium WebDriver

Java Class Library

The Java Class Library is known as Java Application Programming Interface (API) which provides programmers with a collection of prewritten classes. Each prewritten class helps support the logic of a program by supplying useful functions. One of the packages called java.lang is automatically imported into all programs. Therefore classes such as System is employed automatically when using the print () and println () methods to display information. According to Oracle, the following shows four of many Java Class Libraries:

- java.lang – Provides classes that are fundamental to the design of the Java programming language.

- java.io - Provides for system input and output through data streams, serialization and the file system.

- java.math - Provides classes for performing arbitrary-precision integer arithmetic (BigInteger) and arbitrary-precision decimal arithmetic (BigDecimal).

- java.sql - Provides the API for accessing and processing data stored in a data source (usually a relational database) using the Java^{TM} programming language.

Note: Package java.lang contains a math class which is different from package java.math. The math class within java.lang contains methods that performs basic numeric operations.

Chapter 5 described packages in Java. Each package contains a group of related classes. The classes are accessed by the package name. An import statement must be placed in the program in order for a class to utilize members of another class. Chapter 6 will look into interfaces which is a group of related methods.

3 Tips To Master Selenium Within 30 Days
http://tinyurl.com/3-Tips-For-Selenium

Free Webinars, Videos, and Live Trainings
http://tinyurl.com/Free-QTP-UFT-Selenium

Chapter 6
Interfaces

An interface is a collection of related methods. Interfaces are comparable to a class whereby it contains variables and methods. However by default, an interface's variable is declared public, static, and final while the method is declared abstract. It is possible for an interface to perform a task but usually there is no behavior implementation. In other words, most methods in an interface do not contain a body. Therefore an interface method without a body only includes a method's signature. As a result, the interface defines what task to perform but not how to perform the task. The class which implements the interface decides how to perform the task. Interfaces can extend one or more interfaces similar to a subclass extending a superclass. The following is the syntax for an interface:

Syntax
accessmodifier **interface** interfaceName **extends** interfaceName1, interfaceName2, interfaceNameN
{
      variableType variableName1;
      variableType variableName2;
      variableType variableNameN;

      methodType methodName1 (parameter-list);
      methodType methodName2 (parameter-list);
      methodType methodNameN (parameter-list);
}

Syntax Details

Skype: rex.jones34
Twitter: @RexJonesII
Email: Rex.Jones@Test4Success.org
LinkedIn: https://www.linkedin.com/in/rexjones34

Chapter 6
Interfaces

Argument	Description
accessmodifier	Can be public or no access modifier. A public declaration indicates the interface can be used by any code. A no access modifier is the default which indicates the interface is only available to members of its package
interface	A keyword used to declare an interface
interfaceName	The name of an interface
extends	An optional keyword that extends one or more interfaces
interfaceName1, 2, N	One or more interfaces separated by a comma that will be extended
variableType variableName1, 2, N;	One or more interface variables
methodType methodName1 (parameter-list);	One or more interface methods

Figure 6.1 – Interface Syntax Details

The following is an interface example:

Chapter 6
Interfaces   (Part 2) Java 4 Selenium WebDriver

```
1   package InterfaceTesting;
2
3   public interface InterfaceTest
4   {
5       public void methodOne();
6       public void methodTwo();
7   }
```

Figure 6.2 – Interface Example

- Line 3 declares an interface by using the keyword "interface" with a "public" access modifier. Therefore the code can be implemented by any class within any package. The name of the interface is called InterfaceTest.
- Lines 5 and 6 are void abstract methods "methodOne and methodTwo". The keyword "abstract" is not needed within an interface. Notice the semi-colon at the end of each method. The semi-colon is placed at the end of the methods because there is no body/implementation.

Chapter six will discuss the following regarding interfaces:

- ✓ Interface Implementation
- ✓ Interface Variables
- ✓ Multiple Inheritance
- ✓ Default Interface Method

Interface Implementation

Interfaces are implemented using keyword "implements" and one or more classes provide implementation for the methods. If a class does not implement a method by providing a body then the class must be declared as abstract. Each class may implement the same interface differently while supporting the same methods. It is important to know that one class can

Skype: rex.jones34
Twitter: @RexJonesII
Email: Rex.Jones@Test4Success.org
LinkedIn: https://www.linkedin.com/in/rexjones34

Chapter 6
Interfaces   (Part 2) Java 4 Selenium WebDriver
implement multiple interfaces. The following is the syntax for a class implementing an interface:

Syntax
class ClassName **extends** SuperClassName **implements** interfaceName
{
     // Class Body
}

The following is an example of a class implementing an interface.

```
1  package InterfaceTesting;
2
3  public interface InterfaceTest
4  {
5      public void methodOne();
6      public void methodTwo();
7  }
8
```

```
1  package InterfaceTesting;
2
3  public class InterfaceExamples implements InterfaceTest
4  {
5      public void methodOne()
6      {
7          System.out.println("This is the body which implements methodOne");
8      }
9      public void methodTwo()
10     {
11         System.out.println("This is the body which implements methodTwo");
12     }
13
14     public static void main(String[] args)
15     {
16         InterfaceTest objInterface = new InterfaceExamples();
17         objInterface.methodTwo();
18     }
19 }
```

Figure 6.3 – Class Implements An Interface

Program Output:
```
This is the body which implements methodTwo
```

Note: The screenshot displays a split image due to the interface and class being in separate files. Eclipse displays a message which states "interface must be defined in its own file" if the interface and class is located in the same file.

3 Tips To Master Selenium Within 30 Days
http://tinyurl.com/3-Tips-For-Selenium

Free Webinars, Videos, and Live Trainings
http://tinyurl.com/Free-QTP-UFT-Selenium

- Line 3 includes the "implements" keyword within the class definition
- Lines 5 – 12 are the implemented methods which has a body. Each class method must match the interface method. Therefore the methods are declared "public", "void" method type, and same signature. The class would have been declared as abstract if one of the methods were not implemented. An abstract class resembles the following declaration:

abstract public class InterfaceExamples **implements** InterfaceTest

Interface Variables

Interface constants (known as constants) are implicitly declared as public, static, and final. In other words, interface variables are by default constants initialized with a value. Constants are unchangeable values assigned to a variable name. The values are established in an interface without a method and shared across all files. A class implements the interface variables in the same manner as methods. The following is an example of an interface variable:

Skype: rex.jones34
Twitter: @RexJonesII
Email: Rex.Jones@Test4Success.org
LinkedIn: https://www.linkedin.com/in/rexjones34

Chapter 6
Interfaces   (Part 2) Java 4 Selenium WebDriver

```
1  package InterfaceTesting;
2
3  public interface InterfaceVariable
4  {
5      int DAYS_PER_WEEK = 7;
6      int MAX_HOURS_PER_DAY = 24;
7  }
8
```

Figure 6.4 – Interface Variable Example

Multiple Inheritance

Multiple inheritance is when an interface extends another interface or a class implements multiple interfaces. The keyword "extends" is used to extend an interface. An extension of interfaces is beneficial if a programmer elects to add more methods. Errors are displayed if a method is added to the original interface and the interface has already been implemented by a class. All of the classes which used the original interface will break existing code because there is no implementation of the newly added method. However the original interface can get extended to accommodate the new method in a separate interface. Programmers can decide to either continue using the original interface or start using the extended interface.

A class inherits multiple interfaces by using the keyword "implements" followed by the interfaces which are separated using a comma. A class must provide implementations for all methods if the interface inherits another interface or the class implements multiple interfaces. The following is an example of multiple inheritance for an interface:

Chapter 6
Interfaces   (Part 2) Java 4 Selenium WebDriver

```
1  package InterfaceTesting;
2
3  public interface ExtendInterface extends InterfaceTest
4  {
5      public void methodThree();
6      public void methodFour();
7  }
```

Figure 6.5 – Interface Extend Example

- Line 3 uses the "extends" keyword to extends an interface "InterfaceTest". The extended interface contains abstract methods "methodOne and methodTwo" from Figure 6.2 Interface Example

- Lines 5 and 6 display public void abstract methods "methodThree and methodFour". The methods from the extended interface are not needed when inheriting an interface. Additional interfaces can be extended by adding the interface name and separating all interfacing with a comma

The following is an example of a class implementing multiple interfaces:

Skype: rex.jones34
Twitter: @RexJonesII
Email: Rex.Jones@Test4Success.org
LinkedIn: https://www.linkedin.com/in/rexjones34

Chapter 6
Interfaces   (Part 2) Java 4 Selenium WebDriver

```java
1  package InterfaceTesting;
2
3  public class MultipleInterfaces implements InterfaceTest, ExtendInterface
4  {
5      public void methodOne()
6      {
7          System.out.println("This is the body which implements methodOne");
8      }
9      public void methodTwo()
10     {
11         System.out.println("This is the body which implements methodTwo");
12     }
13
14     public void methodThree()
15     {
16         System.out.println("This is the body which implements methodThree");
17     }
18     public void methodFour()
19     {
20         System.out.println("This is the body which implements methodFour");
21     }
22
23     public static void main(String[] args)
24     {
25         InterfaceTest objInterface1 = new MultipleInterfaces();
26         objInterface1.methodOne();
27
28         ExtendInterface objInterface3 = new MultipleInterfaces();
29         objInterface3.methodThree();
30     }
31 }
```

Figure 6.6 – Class Implementing Multiple Interfaces

Program Output:
```
This is the body which implements methodOne
This is the body which implements methodThree
```

- Line 3 uses the "implements" keyword to implement multiple interfaces "InterfaceTest and ExtendInterface"
- Lines 5 – 21 implements a body/behavior for each method defined in both interfaces

3 Tips To Master Selenium Within 30 Days
http://tinyurl.com/3-Tips-For-Selenium

Free Webinars, Videos, and Live Trainings
http://tinyurl.com/Free-QTP-UFT-Selenium

- Lines 25 – 29 create objects "objInterface1 and objInterface3" that is used to call methods "methodOne and methodThree"

Default Interface Method

A default interface method (known an extension method) allows an interface method to provide a body. Therefore, the interface methods are permitted to implement a behavior. This change occurred in the release of JDK 8 whereby an interface has the option to remain abstract or define a default implementation. Default methods contain a "default" keyword which precedes the method type. An advantage of default methods is a class does not require implementation. However a class requires implementation of a default method if a different value is returned. The following is an example of a default method using figures "Figures 6.2 – Interface Example and Figure 6.5 – Interface Extend Example".

```
1  package InterfaceTesting;
2
3  public interface DefaultMethod
4  {
5      public void methodOne();
6      public void methodTwo();
7
8      default public void methodThree()
9      {
10         System.out.println("This is the body which implements methodThree");
11     }
12     default public void methodFour()
13     {
14         System.out.println("This is the body which implements methodFour");
15     }
16 }
```

Figure 6.7 – Default Method Example

Skype: rex.jones34
Twitter: @RexJonesII
Email: Rex.Jones@Test4Success.org
LinkedIn: https://www.linkedin.com/in/rexjones34

Chapter 6
Interfaces   (Part 2) Java 4 Selenium WebDriver
Chapter 6 explained interfaces which is a collection of related methods. Generally, the interface methods do not contain a body. Therefore the interface methods define what task to perform but not how to perform the task. However, a default method allows an interface method to provide a body which occurred in the release of JDK 8. Chapter 7 will discuss errors, exceptions, and debugging.

3 Tips To Master Selenium Within 30 Days
http://tinyurl.com/3-Tips-For-Selenium

Free Webinars, Videos, and Live Trainings
http://tinyurl.com/Free-QTP-UFT-Selenium

Chapter 7
Errors, Exceptions, and Debugging

All programs will include some kind of error. An error is an unwanted problem in the program. It can be an unexpected problem such as misspelling a keyword. In Java, the errors are grouped into three types:

1. <u>Syntax</u> – prevents code from executing
2. <u>Runtime</u> – generates an error when the program is executing
3. <u>Logical</u> – does not generate an error message due to a fault in the code's logic

<u>Logical errors</u> are difficult to locate because an error message is not generated. Usually, logical errors are hidden until a programmer debugs their program. Although errors are unavoidable problems, some problems can be handled at runtime. Problems handled at runtime are called exceptions. The programmer creates a block of code called an exception handler which handle exceptions in a disciplined manner. A benefit of handling exceptions is the program continues to run after catching the exception.

<u>Debugging</u> is a process that allows a programmer to observe then correct an error. The problems in a program can be found by using System.*out*.print, System.*out*.println or a debugger. A debugger is a tool that follows a code's logic. Most programmers prefer to use a debugger instead of several print statements to investigate a problem. If print statements are used, then the programmer must add the print statements and remove the print statement after resolving the problem.

Chapter seven will explain the following regarding errors, exceptions, and debugging.

✓ <u>Error Types</u>
✓ <u>Throwable Exception Parent Class</u>
✓ <u>Java's Built-In Exceptions</u>

Skype: rex.jones34
Twitter: @RexJonesII
Email: Rex.Jones@Test4Success.org
LinkedIn: https://www.linkedin.com/in/rexjones34

Chapter 7
Errors, Exceptions, and Debugging   (Part 2) Java 4 Selenium WebDriver

Error Types

In programming, errors are problems that result from a mistake in a programmer's code. The errors are found before a program executes, when a program executes, and sometimes hidden within a program. The errors located before execution of a program are called syntax errors. Errors found during execution of a program are called runtime errors. The hardest errors to discover which are hidden in a program are called logical errors. Nevertheless, all errors must be resolved to have a successful program.

Syntax Errors

Syntax errors (known as compiler errors) stop programs from executing. Recall from the first book "*Part 1 – Java 4 Selenium WebDriver*", syntax is a set of rules that specifies a structured combination of words and symbols. If not structured correctly, an error occurs to prevent the statements from compiling. As a result, the errors are not compiled due to an inaccuracy in the programmer's code.

Syntax errors are the easiest errors to locate and resolve. An Integrated Development Environment (IDE) such as Eclipse points out the errors. The errors are disclosed by a red underline beneath the code and/or red X to the left of a line number. In addition, a tool tip displays a message that reveals the error after hovering over the red X. According to

3 Tips To Master Selenium Within 30 Days
http://tinyurl.com/3-Tips-For-Selenium

Free Webinars, Videos, and Live Trainings
http://tinyurl.com/Free-QTP-UFT-Selenium

Chapter 7
Errors, Exceptions, and Debugging   (Part 2) Java 4 Selenium WebDriver
Beginning Java® Programming (2015), syntax errors include the following examples (page 172):

> ➢ Misspelled class, variable, or method names
> ➢ Misspelled keywords
> ➢ Missing semicolons
> ➢ Missing return type for methods
> ➢ Out of place or mismatched parentheses and brackets
> ➢ Undeclared or uninitialized variables
> ➢ Incorrect format of loops, methods, or other structures

The following code has syntax errors in the program:

```java
1  package Errors;
2
3  public class SyntaxError
4  {
5      public static void main(String[] args)
6      {
7          int x, y, total;
8
9          x = 10;
10         y = 6,
11         Total = x + y;
12
13         System.out.println("The total of 10 + 6 is " + total);
14     }
15 }
```

Figure 7.1 – Syntax Error Example

- Line 10 displays an error due to a comma rather than a semi-colon

Skype: rex.jones34
Twitter: @RexJonesII
Email: Rex.Jones@Test4Success.org
LinkedIn: https://www.linkedin.com/in/rexjones34

Chapter 7
Errors, Exceptions, and Debugging   (Part 2) Java 4 Selenium WebDriver

- Line 11 displays an error because Total is not declared. Line 7 declares total but the first letter begins with a lowercase "t" rather than an uppercase "T".

The following is an example of Eclipse revealing the error after hovering over the red X for line 10:

```
1  package Errors;
2
3  public class SyntaxError                          Syntax error on token ",", ; expected
4  {
5      public static void main(String[] args)
6      {
7          int x, y, total;
8
9          x = 10;
10  Multiple markers at this line
11    - Line breakpoint:SyntaxError [line: 10] - main(String[])
12    - Syntax error on token ",", ; expected
13          System.out.println("The total of 10 + 6 is " + total);
14      }
15  }
```

Figure 7.2 – Error Message After Hovering Over Red X

The error states "Syntax error on token ",", ; expected" which means the compiler expects a semi-colon. A gray X with a circle and white background appears after correcting the error. Consequently, the red underline and red X disappear after replacing the comma with a semi-colon to complete the statement.

Some errors display a yellow circle with a smaller red X similar to line 11. This error uncovers multiple solutions that may resolve the problem after clicking the red X. The following is a screenshot of Eclipse displaying possible solutions to fix the error on line 11:

3 Tips To Master Selenium Within 30 Days
http://tinyurl.com/3-Tips-For-Selenium

Free Webinars, Videos, and Live Trainings
http://tinyurl.com/Free-QTP-UFT-Selenium

Chapter 7
Errors, Exceptions, and Debugging   (Part 2) Java 4 Selenium WebDriver

```
 1  package Errors;
 2
 3  public class SyntaxError
 4  {
 5      public static void main(String[] args)
 6      {
 7          int x, y, total;
 8
 9          x = 10;
10          y = 6;
11          Total = x + y;
12
13          S  ⟲ Change to 'total'              is " + total);
            ◉ Create local variable 'Total'
14      }      ▢ Create field 'Total'
15  }          ◉ Create parameter 'Total'
16            ✖ Remove assignment
17            ⟲ Change to 'x'
18            ⟲ Change to 'y'
19            ⌶ Rename in file (Ctrl+2, R)
20
```

Figure 7.3 – Possible Solutions After Clicking The Red X

Several solutions unfold after clicking the red X on line 11. However, the correct solution is the first option "Change to 'total'". Eclipse automatically updates the code to reflect the selected proposed solution. Therefore lines 10 and 11 display a gray X with a circle and white background. Both X's are removed after saving the file.

Runtime Errors
Runtime errors are detected when a program executes an invalid action. Invalid actions are operations such as divide by zero. The syntax is correct so the program runs but a problem occurs during runtime. The following is an example of a runtime error:

Skype: rex.jones34
Twitter: @RexJonesII
Email: Rex.Jones@Test4Success.org
LinkedIn: https://www.linkedin.com/in/rexjones34

Chapter 7
Errors, Exceptions, and Debugging   (Part 2) Java 4 Selenium WebDriver

```java
1  package Errors;
2
3  public class RuntimeError
4  {
5      public static void main(String[] args)
6      {
7          int a, b, x, y;
8          int result, sum;
9
10         a = x = 10;
11         b = y = 0;
12
13         result = a/b;
14         sum = x+y;
15
16         System.out.println("What is 10/0?" + result);
17         System.out.println("What is 10+0?" + sum);
18     }
19 }
```

Figure 7.4 – Runtime Error Example

Program Output:
```
Exception in thread "main" java.lang.ArithmeticException: / by zero
    at Errors.RuntimeError.main(RuntimeError.java:13)
```

Figure 7.5 – Console/Program Output Screenshot

- Line 7 declares four variables "a, b, x, y"

3 Tips To Master Selenium Within 30 Days
http://tinyurl.com/3-Tips-For-Selenium

Free Webinars, Videos, and Live Trainings
http://tinyurl.com/Free-QTP-UFT-Selenium

Chapter 7
Errors, Exceptions, and Debugging   (Part 2) Java 4 Selenium WebDriver

- Line 8 declares two variables "result, sum"
- Line 10 initialize two of the variables "a and b" to 10
- Line 11 initialize two of the variables "x and y" to 0
- Line 13 initialize variable "result" to divide 'a' by 'b'
- Line 14 initialize variable sum to add 'x' plus 'y'

The program executes but a runtime error occurs due to line 13. Therefore execution immediately stops and does not execute lines 14 – 17. Although, line 14 is a valid operation, the compiler will not execute the statement. The Program Output displays a message which informs the programmer of the problem. First line indicates a problem by showing "/ by zero" meaning a number was divided by zero. Second line specifies where the problem occurred by showing the package name "Errors", class name "RuntimeError", method name "main", and line number "13".

Logical Errors

Logical errors execute without an error but logically performs the wrong task. As a result, this type of error is challenging unless a programmer knows what to expect. The actual results are compared to the expected results to verify what went wrong. Logical errors such as using an operator precedence incorrectly or misplacing a semicolon will execute and produce improper results. The following are examples of logical errors:

Skype: rex.jones34
Twitter: @RexJonesII
Email: Rex.Jones@Test4Success.org
LinkedIn: https://www.linkedin.com/in/rexjones34

Chapter 7
Errors, Exceptions, and Debugging   (Part 2) Java 4 Selenium WebDriver

```java
1  package Errors;
2
3  public class LogicalErrors
4  {
5      public static void main(String[] args)
6      {
7          int total1 = (9 + (8 * 7)) / 6;
8          int total2 = (9 + 8) * (7 / 6);
9          int total3 = 9 + 8 * 7 / 6;
10         int total4 = (9 + 8) * 7 / 6;
11
12         System.out.println("What is the result of total1: " + total1);
13         System.out.println("What is the result of total2: " + total2);
14         System.out.println("What is the result of total3: " + total3);
15         System.out.println("What is the result of total4: " + total4);
16      }
17 }
```

Figure 7.6 – Operator Precedence Logical Error Example

Program Output:

```
What is the result of total1: 10
What is the result of total2: 17
What is the result of total3: 18
What is the result of total4: 19
```

Lines 7 – 10 initialize each variable "total1, total2, total3, total4" with a different operator precedence. Each variable produce a different value although the values "9, 8, 7, 6" are the same. The following is an example of misplacing a semicolon:

Chapter 7
Errors, Exceptions, and Debugging   (Part 2) Java 4 Selenium WebDriver

```java
1  package Errors;
2
3  public class LogicalErrors2
4  {
5      public static void main(String[] args)
6      {
7          int i;
8
9          for (i = 0; i < 5; i++);
10         {
11             System.out.println("The loop control variable is " + i);
12         }
13     }
14 }
```

Figure 7.7 – Misplaced Semicolon Logical Error Example

Program Output:
The loop control variable is 5

Line 9 incorrectly places a semicolon at the end of the for loop. Therefore the program outputs 5 rather than 0, 1, 2, 3, 4.

Throwable Exception Parent Class

An exception is a Java class whereby java.lang.Throwable is the parent class. Therefore, the Throwable exception represents all exception classes. An object of a particular exception class is generated when an exception is thrown in a program. There are two main subclasses deriving from the Throwable parent class:

1. **Error** – contains serious exceptions that occur in the Java Virtual Machine (JVM). JVM is a machine within a machine which solves problems and helps the program

Skype: rex.jones34
Twitter: @RexJonesII
Email: Rex.Jones@Test4Success.org
LinkedIn: https://www.linkedin.com/in/rexjones34

Chapter 7
Errors, Exceptions, and Debugging   (Part 2) Java 4 Selenium WebDriver
   remain secure. An Error subclass is not managed by the programmer.

2. **Exception** – contains exceptions that occur in the program. An Exception subclass is
   managed by the programmer.

This book "*Part 2 – Java 4 Selenium WebDriver*" will explain the Exception subclass.
Exceptions from subclass "Error" are beyond a programmer's control. The following is a
diagram from Program Creek which shows a hierarchy of Java Exception classes:

Chapter 7
Errors, Exceptions, and Debugging   (Part 2) Java 4 Selenium WebDriver

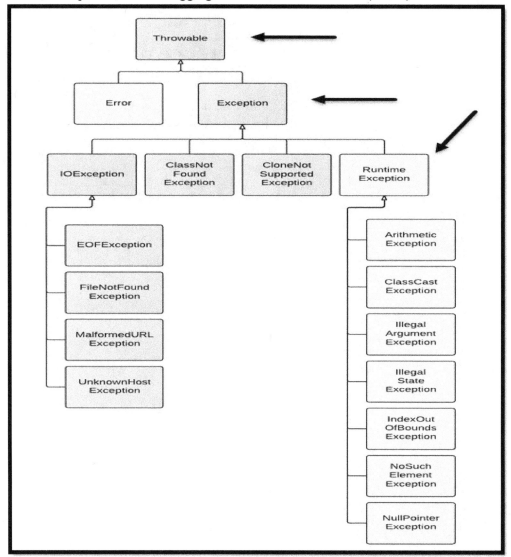

Figure 7.8 – Java Exception Class Hierarchy

Skype: rex.jones34
Twitter: @RexJonesII
Email: Rex.Jones@Test4Success.org
LinkedIn: https://www.linkedin.com/in/rexjones34

Chapter 7
Errors, Exceptions, and Debugging   (Part 2) Java 4 Selenium WebDriver

Java's Built-In Exceptions

In Java, there is a respectable amount of exception classes defined inside the java.lang standard package. Therefore some exceptions are automatically available due to an implicit import of java.lang into every program. Most of the exceptions are subclasses that originate from a standard type called RuntimeException. RuntimeException contains exceptions that are not checked by the compiler. All other exceptions are checked by the compiler and must be included in a method's throws list. The following is a list of unchecked and checked exceptions defined in the java.lang package:

Unchecked Exceptions	Description
ArithmeticException	Arithmetic error, such as divide-by-zero.
ArrayIndexOutOfBoundsException	Array index is out-of-bounds.
ArrayStoreException	Assignment to an array element of an incompatible type.
ClassCastException	Invalid cast.
EnumConstantNotPresentException	An attempt is made to use an undefined enumeration value.
IllegalArgumentException	Illegal argument used to invoke a method.
IllegalMonitorStateException	Illegal monitor operation, such as waiting on an unlocked thread.
IllegalStateException	Environment or application is in incorrect state.
IllegalThreadStateException	Requested operation not compatible with current thread state.
IndexOutOfBoundsException	Some type of index is out-of-bounds.

Chapter 7
Errors, Exceptions, and Debugging   (Part 2) Java 4 Selenium WebDriver

NegativeArraySizeException	Array created with a negative size.
NullPointerException	Invalid use of a null reference.
NumberFormatException	Invalid conversion of a string to a numeric format.
SecurityException	Attempt to violate security.
StringIndexOutOfBoundsException	Attempt to index outside the bounds of a string.
TypeNotPresentException	Type not found.
UnsupportedOperationException	An unsupported operation was encountered.

Figure 7.9 – Java Unchecked Exceptions

Checked Exceptions	Description
ClassNotFoundException	Class not found.
CloneNotSupportedException	Attempt to clone an object that does not implement the Cloneable interface.
IllegalAccessException	Access to a class is denied.
InstantiationException	Attempt to create an object of an abstract class or interface.
InterruptedException	One thread has been interrupted by another thread.
NoSuchFieldException	A requested field does not exist.
NoSuchMethodException	A requested method does not exist.

Skype: rex.jones34
Twitter: @RexJonesII
Email: Rex.Jones@Test4Success.org
LinkedIn: https://www.linkedin.com/in/rexjones34

Chapter 7
Errors, Exceptions, and Debugging   (Part 2) Java 4 Selenium WebDriver

ReflectiveOperationException	Superclass of reflection-related exceptions.

Figure 7.10 – Java Checked Exceptions

<u>Note</u>: In addition to java.lang, the following packages include exceptions:

java.awt	java.net
java.awt.color	java.rmi
java.awt.datatransfer	java.security
java.beans	java.text

Figure 7.11 – Packages That Include Exceptions

Common Exceptions

Common exceptions are exceptions that occur frequently in a program. These type of exception happens to new programmers as well as experienced programmers. The following is a list of common exceptions in alphabetical order:

- ArrayIndexOutOfBoundsException
- ClassCastException
- IllegalArgumentException
- IllegalStateException
- NullPointerException
- NumberFormatException
- OutOfMemoryError
- StackOverFlowError

Arrays start at index position zero which stores the first value. Therefore the last index position is one less the size of the complete array. An ArrayIndexOutOfBoundsException is

3 Tips To Master Selenium Within 30 Days
http://tinyurl.com/3-Tips-For-Selenium

Free Webinars, Videos, and Live Trainings
http://tinyurl.com/Free-QTP-UFT-Selenium

Chapter 7
Errors, Exceptions, and Debugging   (Part 2) Java 4 Selenium WebDriver
thrown when a program attempts to access an index outside the boundaries of the array. The
following is an ArrayIndexOutOfBoundsException:

```java
1  package ExceptionHandling;
2
3  public class CommonException
4  {
5
6      public static void main(String[] args)
7      {
8          String[] continents = new String[7];
9
10         continents[0] = "Africa";
11         continents[1] = "Antarctica";
12         continents[2] = "Asia";
13         continents[3] = "Australia";
14         continents[4] = "Europe";
15         continents[5] = "North America";
16         continents[6] = "South America";
17         continents[7] = "America";          ⬅
18
19         System.out.println("There are " + continents.length + " countries");
20     }
21 }
```

Figure 7.12 – ArrayIndexOutOfBoundsException / Common Exception Example

- Line 8 creates an array with 7 elements "String[] continents = **new** String[7];"
- Line 17 which contains "continents[7] = "America";" is out of bounds for the array "continents"
- Line 19 is not executed because the error causes the program to stop

Program Output:
```
Exception in thread "main" java.lang.ArrayIndexOutOfBoundsException: 7
    at ExceptionHandling.CommonException.main(CommonException.java:17)
```

According to the Program Output, the out of bounds index is "7" located at line 17. The first
line indicates there is an exception then shows the exception type

Skype: rex.jones34
Twitter: @RexJonesII
Email: Rex.Jones@Test4Success.org
LinkedIn: https://www.linkedin.com/in/rexjones34

Chapter 7
Errors, Exceptions, and Debugging   (Part 2) Java 4 Selenium WebDriver
"`java.lang.ArrayIndexOutOfBoundsException`". Number 7 specifies the index which
causes the exception. The second line displays where the exception is located " `at`
`ExceptionHandling.CommonException.main(`CommonException.java:17`)`". The
following is a translation of the second line:

An exception occurred in package name "ExceptionHandling", class name
"CommonException", method name "main", at line number 17.

Principles of Handling Exceptions

It is understood that exceptions are problems that occur at runtime (during program
execution). Java allows an exception handler to handle exceptions which include benefits.
Remember the runtime error example from Figure 7.4, where execution stopped due to a
division by zero. A benefit of handling exceptions is the program will continue executing
after responding to an error. Therefore an error does not stop program execution but the
exception handler permits the program to continue running. In Java, there are five
interrelated keywords that facilitate the management of handling exceptions. The following is
a description of each keyword:

1. try – monitors code where an exception might occur
2. catch – handles the exception when an error occurs
3. throw – manually throws a custom exception
4. throws – throws an exception that occurred from a method
5. finally – automatically executes code after exiting a try block

The Java Virtual Machine (JVM) catches all exceptions if the exception handler does not
catch the exception. JVM displays an error message which is good for debugging but not for
handling exceptions. It is not good for handling exceptions due to termination of the
program.

3 Tips To Master Selenium Within 30 Days
http://tinyurl.com/3-Tips-For-Selenium

Free Webinars, Videos, and Live Trainings
http://tinyurl.com/Free-QTP-UFT-Selenium

Chapter 7
Errors, Exceptions, and Debugging   (Part 2) Java 4 Selenium WebDriver

Try / Catch Block

The try / catch block allows code to be tried to verify whether an exception occurs. If an exception occurs then the exception is caught to specify what should happen. The keywords "try and catch" operate together when handling exceptions. Try is used to contain the code that may cause an exception while catch manages the exception. Both keywords "try and catch" are central to handling exceptions. A try block is provided along with one or more catch blocks. It is important to know that the try block and all catch blocks are bypassed if no exception occurs. The following is the try / catch block syntax for handling exceptions:

Syntax
```
try
{
   // Code monitored by try block
}
 catch (ExceptionType1 excObject)
{
   // Exception Handler for ExceptionType1
}
catch (ExceptionType2 excObject)
{
   // Exception Handler for ExceptionType2
}
```

The following is the syntax details for try and catch block:

Arguments	Description
try	Monitors a block of code for an exception
catch	Handles and processes the exception

Skype: rex.jones34
Twitter: @RexJonesII
Email: Rex.Jones@Test4Success.org
LinkedIn: https://www.linkedin.com/in/rexjones34

Chapter 7
Errors, Exceptions, and Debugging   (Part 2) Java 4 Selenium WebDriver

ExceptionType1 ExceptionType2	Type of exception that must be the name of a class inherited from the Throwable class
excObject	Receives the value of an exception caught by the handler.

Figure 7.13 – Syntax Details

The following is an example of a try and catch exception handler:

```java
1  package ExceptionHandling;
2
3  public class TryCatchBlock
4  {
5      public static void main(String[] args)
6      {
7          String[] continents = new String[7];
8          try          ⬅
9          {
10             System.out.println("An exception has not been thrown");
11
12             continents[0] = "Africa";
13             continents[1] = "Antarctica";
14             continents[2] = "Asia";
15             continents[3] = "Australia";
16             continents[4] = "Europe";
17             continents[5] = "North America";
18             continents[6] = "South America";
19             continents[7] = "America";
20
21             System.out.println("There are " + continents.length + " continents");
22         }
23         catch (ArrayIndexOutOfBoundsException exc)    ⬅
24         {
25             System.out.println("Exception!!! - Array Index Out of Bounds. Not a valid continent");
26         }
27         System.out.println("This line executes automatically whether an exception occurs or not");
28     }
29 }
```

Figure 7.14 – Try and Catch Block Example

Program Output:
An exception has not been thrown

3 Tips To Master Selenium Within 30 Days
http://tinyurl.com/3-Tips-For-Selenium

Free Webinars, Videos, and Live Trainings
http://tinyurl.com/Free-QTP-UFT-Selenium

Chapter 7
Errors, Exceptions, and Debugging   (Part 2) Java 4 Selenium WebDriver

```
Exception!!! - Array Index Out of Bounds. Not a valid continent
This line executes automatically whether an exception occurs or not
```

- Line 8 starts the code monitoring process for errors using the try block
- Line 19 forces an exception when defining index position 7 which is outside of the array boundaries. Therefore the try block is terminated and the program transfers control to the catch block
- Line 21 does not execute due to the exception at line 19
- Line 23 starts the exception handling process by listing the exception type "ArrayIndexOutOfBoundsException" within the catch block
- Line 25 is executed within the catch block after the exception is caught
- Line 27 is executed following the catch block. This line executes automatically whether an exception occurs or not.

A common practice in Java is to associate multiple catch blocks with a try block. Each catch block must include a unique exception type such as arithmetic exception, array index out of bounds exception, etc. The exception type determines which catch block is executed after creating multiple catch blocks. Therefore if the arithmetic exception type is executed then the array index out of bounds exception type is bypassed. The following is an example of a try block with multiple catch blocks:

Skype: rex.jones34
Twitter: @RexJonesII
Email: Rex.Jones@Test4Success.org
LinkedIn: https://www.linkedin.com/in/rexjones34

Chapter 7
Errors, Exceptions, and Debugging   (Part 2) Java 4 Selenium WebDriver

```
1  package ExceptionHandling;
2
3  public class MultipleCatchBlocks
4  {
5      public static void main(String[] args)
6      {
7          int oddNumbers[] = {11, 33, 55, 77, 99, 111};
8          int evenNumbers[] = {0, 2, 4, 6, 8};
9
10         for (int i = 0; i < oddNumbers.length; i++)
11         {
12             try
13             {
14                 System.out.println("What is " + oddNumbers[i] + "/" + evenNumbers[i] + "? "
15                     + "" + oddNumbers[i]/evenNumbers[i]);
16             }
17             catch (ArithmeticException except)
18             {
19                 System.out.println("Exception!!! - Cannot divide a number by zero");
20             }
21             catch (ArrayIndexOutOfBoundsException except)
22             {
23                 System.out.println("Exception!!! - Cannot locate the index");
24             }
25         }
26     }
27 }
```

Figure 7.15 – Multiple Catch Blocks

Program Output:
```
Exception!!! - Cannot divide a number by zero
What is 33/2? 16
What is 55/4? 13
What is 77/6? 12
What is 99/8? 12
Exception!!! - Cannot locate the index
```

- Line 17 displays the first catch block which contains an arithmetic exception. Catch blocks are evaluated according to their order of association to the try block. Therefore

3 Tips To Master Selenium Within 30 Days
http://tinyurl.com/3-Tips-For-Selenium

Free Webinars, Videos, and Live Trainings
http://tinyurl.com/Free-QTP-UFT-Selenium

Chapter 7
Errors, Exceptions, and Debugging   (Part 2) Java 4 Selenium WebDriver

this catch block is evaluated first since it occurs first in the program. The other catch block is ignored when a match is found for this exception type.

- Line 19 is executed when the code reaches zero "0" in array "evenNumbers[]"
- Line 21 displays the second catch block which contains an array index out of bounds exception
- Line 23 is executed when the code searches for an index that is not available in array "evenNumbers[]". The other catch block is ignored when a match is found for this exception type.

Finally Block

The finally block is an extension of try / catch block. This block confirms certain actions such as writing data to a file is performed whether an exception occurs or not. Java allows the same action to be placed within the try block and catch block. On the other hand, placing the same code in both blocks "try block and catch block" creates duplicate code.

For example, what happens if there is no exception and data needs to be written to a file. In this scenario, the try block executes the code while the catch block is bypassed. However, if there is an exception, the catch block executes the code while the try block is bypassed. Therefore, a programmer must place code in the try and catch block for certainty that data is written to a file. In programming, it is difficult to read and maintain duplicate code. A finally block is not required but it will certainly write data to the file when an exception is thrown and when it is not thrown. The following is the syntax of a try/catch/finally block:

Syntax
try
{
    // Code monitored by try block
}
catch (ExceptionType1 excObject)
{
    // Exception Handler for ExceptionType1

Skype: rex.jones34
Twitter: @RexJonesII
Email: Rex.Jones@Test4Success.org
LinkedIn: https://www.linkedin.com/in/rexjones34

Chapter 7
Errors, Exceptions, and Debugging   (Part 2) Java 4 Selenium WebDriver

```
}
catch (ExceptionType2 excObject)
{
    // Exception Handler for ExceptionType2
}
finally
{
    // Execute code if exception occurs or not
}
```

The following is an example using the try/catch/finally block:

Chapter 7
Errors, Exceptions, and Debugging   (Part 2) Java 4 Selenium WebDriver

```java
1  package ExceptionHandling;
2
3  public class FinallyBlock
4  {
5      public static void main(String[] args)
6      {
7          int oddNumbers[] = {11, 33, 55, 77, 99, 111};
8          int evenNumbers[] = {0, 2, 4, 6, 8};
9
10         for (int i = 0; i < oddNumbers.length; i++)
11         {
12             try
13             {
14                 System.out.println("What is " + oddNumbers[i] + "/" + evenNumbers[i] + "? "
15                         + "" + oddNumbers[i]/evenNumbers[i]);
16             }
17             catch (ArithmeticException except)
18             {
19                 System.out.println("Exception!!! - Cannot divide a number by zero");
20             }
21             catch (ArrayIndexOutOfBoundsException except)
22             {
23                 System.out.println("Exception!!! - Cannot locate the index");
24             }
25             finally        ⬅
26             {
27                 System.out.println("   Perform an Action");
28             }
29         }
30     }
31 }
```

Figure 7.16 – Finally Block

Program Output:
```
Exception!!! - Cannot divide a number by zero
   Perform an Action
What is 33/2? 16
   Perform an Action
What is 55/4? 13
   Perform an Action
What is 77/6? 12
   Perform an Action
What is 99/8? 12
```

Skype: rex.jones34
Twitter: @RexJonesII
Email: Rex.Jones@Test4Success.org
LinkedIn: https://www.linkedin.com/in/rexjones34

Chapter 7
Errors, Exceptions, and Debugging   (Part 2) Java 4 Selenium WebDriver

```
    Perform an Action
Exception!!! - Cannot locate the index
    Perform an Action
```

- Line 25 starts the finally block at the end of the try/catch block
- Line 27 is executed automatically when an exception is thrown and when an exception is not thrown

Catch A Throwable Exception

A Throwable exception can be utilized to catch all exceptions since it is the parent class. The superclass Throwable matches all of its subclasses which includes RuntimeException. In order to catch exceptions for both classes, the superclass and subclass must be implemented in their respective catch block. The following is a Throwable superclass and ArithmeticException subclass example using code from Figure 7.15:

Chapter 7
Errors, Exceptions, and Debugging   (Part 2) Java 4 Selenium WebDriver

```java
1  package ExceptionHandling;
2
3  public class SuperSubClassException
4  {
5
6      public static void main(String[] args)
7      {
8          int oddNumbers[] = {11, 33, 55, 77, 99, 111};
9          int evenNumbers[] = {0, 2, 4, 6, 8};
10
11         for (int i = 0; i < oddNumbers.length; i++)
12         {
13             try
14             {
15                 System.out.println("What is " + oddNumbers[i] + "/" + evenNumbers[i] + "? "
16                         + "" + oddNumbers[i]/evenNumbers[i]);
17             }
18             catch (ArithmeticException except)        ⬅
19             {
20                 System.out.println("Exception!!! - Cannot divide a number by zero");
21             }
22             catch (Throwable except)        ⬅
23             {
24                 System.out.println("Exception!!! - The Throwable Exception caught an error");
25             }
26         }
27     }
28 }
```

Figure 7.17 – Throwable and ArithmeticException Example

Program Output:
```
Exception!!! - Cannot divide a number by zero
What is 33/2? 16
What is 55/4? 13
What is 77/6? 12
What is 99/8? 12
Exception!!! - The Throwable Exception caught an error
```

- Line 18 implements the subclass exception "ArithmeticException" inside the first catch block
- Line 20 is executed when the code reaches zero "0" in array "evenNumbers[]"
- Line 22 implements the Throwable exception inside the second catch block

Skype: rex.jones34
Twitter: @RexJonesII
Email: Rex.Jones@Test4Success.org
LinkedIn: https://www.linkedin.com/in/rexjones34

Chapter 7

Errors, Exceptions, and Debugging   (Part 2) Java 4 Selenium WebDriver

- Line 24 is executed when the code searches for an index that is not available in array "evenNumbers[]"

The Throwable superclass and subclass are allowed to catch exceptions by placing the subclass in the first catch block. An error occurs if the Throwable exception is implemented in the first block. The error message states "Unreachable catch block for ArithmeticException. It is already handled by the catch block for Throwable".

Methods Defined By Throwable

As mentioned, Throwable is a superclass of every exception subclass. Therefore all exceptions support methods defined by Throwable. An exception can be caught by a Throwable exception but it is a generic catch. It is best to use a specific exception such as ArithmeticException when handling exceptions. However, some of the methods defined by Throwable can help the superclass be more specific when handling exceptions. The following is a list of Throwable methods:

Method	Description
fillInStackTrace()	Fills in the completed execution stack trace
getLocalizedMessage()	Creates a localized description of the Throwable exception
getMessage()	Returns a detail message of the Throwable exception
printStackTrace()	Prints the stack trace
printStackTrace(PrintStream)	Prints the stack trace to the specified print stream
printStackTrace(PrintWriter)	Prints the stack trace to the specified print writer
toString()	Returns a short exception description after being called by println() method

Figure 7.18 – Methods Defined by Throwable

3 Tips To Master Selenium Within 30 Days
http://tinyurl.com/3-Tips-For-Selenium

Free Webinars, Videos, and Live Trainings
http://tinyurl.com/Free-QTP-UFT-Selenium

Chapter 7
Errors, Exceptions, and Debugging   (Part 2) Java 4 Selenium WebDriver
One of the most common methods defined by Throwable is the printStackTrace() method.
This method prints the stack trace "standard error message". The following is an example of
printStackTrace() method:

```java
1  package ExceptionHandling;
2
3  public class ThrowableMethod
4  {
5      public static void main(String[] args)
6      {
7          int oddNumbers[] = {11, 33, 55, 77, 99, 111};
8          int evenNumbers[] = {0, 2, 4, 6, 8};
9
10         for (int i = 0; i < oddNumbers.length; i++)
11         {
12             try
13             {
14                 System.out.println("What is " + oddNumbers[i] + "/" + evenNumbers[i] + "? "
15                         + "" + oddNumbers[i]/evenNumbers[i]);
16             }
17             catch (ArithmeticException exceptName)
18             {
19                 System.out.println("Exception!!! - Cannot divide a number by zero");
20             }
21             catch (Throwable exceptName)
22             {
23                 System.out.println("Exception!!! - The Throwable Exception caught the following error:" + "\n");
24                 exceptName.printStackTrace();
25             }
26         }
27     }
28 }
```

Figure 7.19 – Print Stack Trace Method

Program Output:
```
Exception!!! - Cannot divide a number by zero
What is 33/2? 16
What is 55/4? 13
What is 77/6? 12
What is 99/8? 12
Exception!!! - The Throwable Exception caught the following error:

java.lang.ArrayIndexOutOfBoundsException: 5
    at ExceptionHandling.ThrowableMethod.main(ThrowableMethod.java:14)
```

Skype: rex.jones34
Twitter: @RexJonesII
Email: Rex.Jones@Test4Success.org
LinkedIn: https://www.linkedin.com/in/rexjones34

Chapter 7
Errors, Exceptions, and Debugging   (Part 2) Java 4 Selenium WebDriver

- Line 21 defines the second catch block with an exception object "exceptName" that will be used to display the exception value
- Line 24 creates the printStackTrace() method by using the exception object followed by the dot operator

Throw vs Throws

The keyword "throw" is used to explicitly throw an exception. An object of the exception parent class Throwable must be created to throw an exception. There are two ways to manually throw an exception:

1. Use a parameter in the catch block
2. Create an object using the new operator

The following is the syntax for manually/explicitly throwing an exception:

Syntax
throw excObject

The following is an example of throwing an exception using the new operator:

3 Tips To Master Selenium Within 30 Days
http://tinyurl.com/3-Tips-For-Selenium

Free Webinars, Videos, and Live Trainings
http://tinyurl.com/Free-QTP-UFT-Selenium

Chapter 7
Errors, Exceptions, and Debugging   (Part 2) Java 4 Selenium WebDriver

```
 1  package ExceptionHandling;
 2
 3  public class ThrowTest
 4  {
 5      int DivideByZero (int num1, int num2)
 6      {
 7          if (num2 == 0)
 8          {
 9              System.out.println("   An error has not been thrown");
10              throw new ArithmeticException ("Exception!!! - Cannot divide a number by zero");
11          }
12          else
13          {
14              return num1/num2;
15          }
16
17      }
18
19      public static void main(String[] args)
20      {
21          try
22          {
23              ThrowTest objThrow = new ThrowTest ();
24              System.out.println(objThrow.DivideByZero(34, 0));
25          }
26          catch (Exception exc)
27          {
28              System.out.println(exc.getMessage());
29          }
30          finally
31          {
32              System.out.println("   Perform an action if exception thrown or not ");
33          }
34      }
35  }
```

Throw a customized exception

Figure 7.20 – Throw Exception Example

Program Output:
```
   An error has not been thrown
Exception!!! - Cannot divide a number by zero
   Perform an action if exception thrown or not
```

- Line 10 creates an explicit exception using keywords "throw" and "new". The keyword "new" is used to construct an instance of "ArithmeticException" with a String parameter.
- Line 24 passes the values "34 and 0" to method "DivideByZero" which starts at line 5. Parameter variable "num2" receives zero "0" which causes the exception
- Line 28 displays the string parameter from line 10 by calling method "getMessage"

Skype: rex.jones34
Twitter: @RexJonesII
Email: Rex.Jones@Test4Success.org
LinkedIn: https://www.linkedin.com/in/rexjones34

Chapter 7
Errors, Exceptions, and Debugging   (Part 2) Java 4 Selenium WebDriver

The keyword "throws" is used to explicitly define exceptions that a method might throw. Therefore, a method call must handle all of the exceptions if a declared method has one or more exceptions using the keyword "throws". The following is an example using "throws" to define an exception list:

Syntax
methodType methodName (parameter-list) throws exc-list
{
    // Method Body
}

The following is an example using "throws" to define an exception:

Chapter 7
Errors, Exceptions, and Debugging   (Part 2) Java 4 Selenium WebDriver

```java
1  package ExceptionHandling;
2
3  public class ThrowsKeywordTest
4  {
5      static void throwMethod () throws NullPointerException
6      {
7          System.out.println("   An error has not been thrown");
8          throw new NullPointerException ("Exception!!! - Null Pointer");
9      }
10
11     public static void main(String[] args)
12     {
13         try
14         {
15             throwMethod ();
16         }
17         catch (NullPointerException exc)
18         {
19             System.out.println("Exception Type " + exc);
20         }
21     }
22 }
```

Figure 7.21 – Throws Exception Example

- Line 5 defines an exception "NullPointerException" using the keyword "throws". Multiple exceptions can be created by way of a comma-separated list of exceptions that the method might throw.
- Line 15 calls method "throwMethod" which has an exception
- Line 19 displays the NullPointerException

Skype: rex.jones34
Twitter: @RexJonesII
Email: Rex.Jones@Test4Success.org
LinkedIn: https://www.linkedin.com/in/rexjones34

Chapter 7
Errors, Exceptions, and Debugging   (Part 2) Java 4 Selenium WebDriver

The following describes the differences between throw and throws:

Throw	Throws
Can throw one exception	Can declare multiple exceptions
Followed by an instance	Followed by an exception class
Used within a method's body	Used within a method's signature

Figure 7.22 – Throw vs Throws

Debugging

At some point while developing a program, the program will consist of errors and/or exceptions. The key for every programmer is to learn how to debug the program. Debugging is the process of detecting and removing unexpected conditions from the program. An IDE such as Eclipse provides a debugger tool which facilitate the debugging process. The tool allows a programmer to execute their code line-by-line to view what is happening on each line.

Breakpoints

To start the debugging process, a breakpoint must be placed in the program. The purpose of breakpoints is to pause execution of the program. As a result, the program runs up to the breakpoint until the debugger receives additional instructions on what to do next. A program can have several breakpoints set or cleared at anytime. The following is a list of ways to set or clear a breakpoint:

1. Double-click the left of the desired line number
2. Move the cursor to the left of the desired line number, right-click the mouse, then select Toggle Breakpoint
3. Move the cursor to the desired line and press shortcut keys (Ctrl + Shift + B)

3 Tips To Master Selenium Within 30 Days
http://tinyurl.com/3-Tips-For-Selenium

Free Webinars, Videos, and Live Trainings
http://tinyurl.com/Free-QTP-UFT-Selenium

Chapter 7
Errors, Exceptions, and Debugging   (Part 2) Java 4 Selenium WebDriver
A blue dot is located next to the line number after setting the breakpoint. Next, the programmer must open the Debug perspective which provides a combination of views and editors to debug a program. The Debug perspective can be opened the following ways:

1. Press F11
2. Right-click inside the program, select Debug As, then Java
3. Click Run then select Debug As, then Java Application
4. Shortcut keys (Alt + Shift + D, J)

Note: Select Yes when Eclipse displays a Confirm Perspective Switch dialogue.

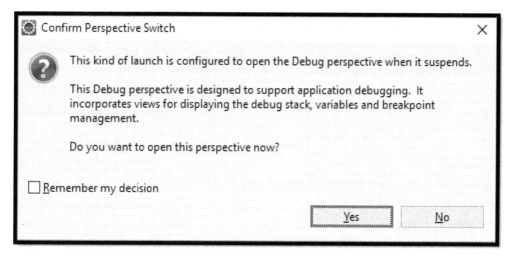

Figure 7.23 – Confirm Perspective Switch Screenshot

The following is a screenshot of the Debug perspective:

Skype: rex.jones34
Twitter: @RexJonesII
Email: Rex.Jones@Test4Success.org
LinkedIn: https://www.linkedin.com/in/rexjones34

Chapter 7
Errors, Exceptions, and Debugging   (Part 2) Java 4 Selenium WebDriver

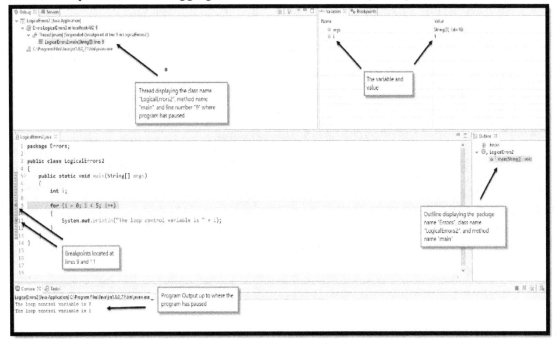

Figure 7.24 – Debug Perspective Screenshot

Step Through The Program

Stepping through the program is when the debugger steps/executes a line of code one line at a time. The process of stepping helps the programmer understand how the logic works. Function keys F5, F6, F7, and F8 control execution of stepping through the program.

- **Step Into** (F5) – Executes only the current code line. The debugger pauses at every line of code that is stepped into including a called method.

3 Tips To Master Selenium Within 30 Days
http://tinyurl.com/3-Tips-For-Selenium

Free Webinars, Videos, and Live Trainings
http://tinyurl.com/Free-QTP-UFT-Selenium

Chapter 7
Errors, Exceptions, and Debugging   (Part 2) Java 4 Selenium WebDriver

- **Step Over** (F6) – Executes the current method without displaying every step. The debugger stays in the main routine while the subroutines execute in the background.

- **Step Return** (F7) – Executes the current method in the background while returning to the method that was stepped into.

- **Resume** (F8) – Executes until the next breakpoint

Chapter 7 discussed errors, exceptions, and debugging. An error is a problem in the program. The three types of errors are syntax, runtime, and logical. Exceptions are errors that occur at runtime. However, an exception handler allows a block of code to manage the exceptions. Therefore the exception allows execution to continue after responding to the problem. Debugging is a process that permits a programmer to detect and resolve all errors. Chapter 8 is an introduction Java's input/output system.

Skype: rex.jones34
Twitter: @RexJonesII
Email: Rex.Jones@Test4Success.org
LinkedIn: https://www.linkedin.com/in/rexjones34

Chapter 8
Utilizing Input and Output

Java's Input/Output (I/O) package "java.io" contains many classes, interfaces, and methods. The package provides input and output streams that reads/writes data. Data is read from an input source and written to an output destination. An input source and output destination is anything that contains information such as a file, string, or memory. Input is data received by the program and output is data sent from the program. A program can be a web browser which receives and sends data.

Chapter eight is an introduction which covers the following regarding Java's large Input/Output system:

- ✓ Streams
- ✓ File Input/Output

Streams

Programs in Java perform input and output through streams. Streams represent a sequence of data that is read or written. Therefore streams have the ability to pass data or perform transformations on data. According to Oracle, the InputStream class is an abstract superclass of all classes representing an input stream of bytes. The OutputStream class is an abstract superclass of all classes representing an output stream of bytes. Therefore the I/O classes is an abstraction that supplies or consumes information. Streams provide a variety of data formats.

3 Tips To Master Selenium Within 30 Days
http://tinyurl.com/3-Tips-For-Selenium

Free Webinars, Videos, and Live Trainings
http://tinyurl.com/Free-QTP-UFT-Selenium

Chapter 8
Utilizing Input and Output   (Part 2) Java 4 Selenium WebDriver
Byte Streams

Byte stream classes are derived from an InputStream and OutputStream. Programs using byte streams provide functionality and manage details of reading/writing. The following is a list of byte stream classes.

Byte Stream	Description
BufferedInputStream	Adds functionality to another input stream-namely, the ability to buffer the input and to support the mark and reset methods
BufferedOutputStream	Implements a buffered output stream
ByteArrayInputStream	Input stream that reads from a byte array
ByteArrayOutputStream	Output stream that writes to a byte array
DataInputStream	An input stream that includes methods for reading the Java standard data types
DataOutputStream	An output stream that includes methods for writing the Java standard data types
FileInputStream	Input stream that reads from a file
FileOutputStream	Output stream that writes to a file
InputStream	Abstract class that is the superclass of all classes representing an input stream of bytes
ObjectInputStream	Input stream for objects
ObjectOutputStream	Output stream for objects
OutputStream	Abstract class that is the superclass of all classes representing an output stream of bytes
PipedInputStream	Provides data bytes that are written to the piped output stream
PipedOutputStream	Connected to a piped input stream to create a communications pipe

Skype: rex.jones34
Twitter: @RexJonesII
Email: Rex.Jones@Test4Success.org
LinkedIn: https://www.linkedin.com/in/rexjones34

Chapter 8
Utilizing Input and Output   (Part 2) Java 4 Selenium WebDriver

PrintStream	Output stream that contains print() and println()
PushbackInputStream	Input stream that allows bytes to be returned to the stream
SequenceInputStream	Represents the logical concatenation of other input streams.

Figure 8.1 – Byte Stream

The following is a list of InputStream methods:

InputStream Method	Description
abstract int read()	Reads the next byte of data from the input stream
boolean markSupported()	Tests if this input stream supports the mark and reset methods
int available ()	Returns an estimate of the number of bytes that can be read (or skipped over) from this input stream without blocking by the next invocation of a method for this input stream
int read (byte[] b)	Reads some number of bytes from the input stream and stores them into the buffer array b
int read (byte[] b, int off, int len)	Reads up to len bytes of data from the input stream into an array of bytes
long skip (long n)	Skips over and discards n bytes of data from this input stream
void close ()	Closes this input stream and releases any system resources associated with the stream
void mark (int readLimit)	Marks the current position in this input stream

3 Tips To Master Selenium Within 30 Days
http://tinyurl.com/3-Tips-For-Selenium

Free Webinars, Videos, and Live Trainings
http://tinyurl.com/Free-QTP-UFT-Selenium

Chapter 8
Utilizing Input and Output   (Part 2) Java 4 Selenium WebDriver

void reset()	Repositions this stream to the position at the time the mark method was last called on this input stream

Figure 8.2 – InputStream Methods

The following is a list of OutputStream methods:

OutputStream Methods	Description
abstract void write(int b)	Writes the specified byte to this output stream
void close()	Closes this output stream and releases any system resources associated with this stream
void flush()	Flushes this output stream and forces any buffered output bytes to be written out
void write(byte[] b)	Writes b.length bytes from the specified byte array to this output stream
void write(byte[] b, int off, int len)	Writes len bytes from the specified byte array starting at offset off to this output stream

Figure 8.3 – OutputStream Methods

Character Stream

Character stream classes are derived from Reader and Writer which offer similar methods as InputStream and OutputStream. The character stream class manages I/O paralleling the byte stream class. Unicode characters are translated from character stream classes. The following is a list of character stream classes:

Character Stream	Description
BufferedReader	Reads text from a character-input stream, buffering characters so as to provide for the efficient reading of characters, arrays, and lines.

Skype: rex.jones34
Twitter: @RexJonesII
Email: Rex.Jones@Test4Success.org
LinkedIn: https://www.linkedin.com/in/rexjones34

BufferedWriter	Writes text to a character-output stream, buffering characters so as to provide for the efficient writing of single characters, arrays, and strings.
CharArrayReader	This class implements a character buffer that can be used as a character-input stream.
CharArrayWriter	This class implements a character buffer that can be used as an Writer.
FileReader	Convenience class for reading character files.
FileWriter	Convenience class for writing character files.
FilterReader	Abstract class for reading filtered character streams
FilterWriter	Abstract class for writing filtered character streams
InputStreamReader	An InputStreamReader is a bridge from byte streams to character streams: It reads bytes and decodes them into characters using a specified charset
LineNumberReader	A buffered character-input stream that keeps track of line numbers
OutputStreamWriter	An OutputStreamWriter is a bridge from character streams to byte streams: Characters written to it are encoded into bytes using a specified charset
PipedReader	Piped character-input streams
PipedWriter	Piped character-output streams.
PrintWriter	Prints formatted representations of objects to a text-output stream.
PushbackReader	A character-stream reader that allows characters to be pushed back into the stream.
Reader	Abstract class for reading character streams
StringReader	A character stream whose source is a string.

Chapter 8
Utilizing Input and Output   (Part 2) Java 4 Selenium WebDriver

StringWriter	A character stream that collects its output in a string buffer, which can then be used to construct a string
Writer	Abstract class for writing to character streams

Figure 8.4 – Character Stream

Buffered Streams

Buffered input streams read data from a memory area known as a buffer. On the other hand, buffered output streams write data to a buffer. In Java, majority of the streams are unbuffered meaning each read or write request is managed directly by the operating system (OS). A management request by an OS make programs less efficient due to a request triggering an expensive operation.

Buffered I/O streams is implemented to reduce overhead by administering a dedicated space in memory. The dedicated space stores data in an efficient manner. For instance, the buffered input stream is only called when the buffer is empty and buffered output streams are only called when the buffer is full. Therefore, the four following buffer classes can be used to wrap around a byte or character I/O stream:

Buffer Classes	Description
BufferedInputStream	Supplies buffering to output streams
BufferedOutputStream	Supplies buffering to input streams
BufferedReader	Reads text from a character input stream

Skype: rex.jones34
Twitter: @RexJonesII
Email: Rex.Jones@Test4Success.org
LinkedIn: https://www.linkedin.com/in/rexjones34

Chapter 8
Utilizing Input and Output   (Part 2) Java 4 Selenium WebDriver

| BufferedWriter | Writes text to a character output stream |

Figure 8.5 – Buffered Streams

Data Streams

Data streams serve as a foundation for String values, binary input, and output of primitive data types such as boolean, byte, char, double, float, int, long, and short. A DataInput or DataOutput interface is implemented by all of the data streams. The DataInput interface provides methods for reading while DataOutput interface provides methods for writing all of Java's primitive types. DataInputStream implements the DataInput interface and DataOutputStream implements the DataOutput interface. The following is a list of methods for DataInputStream and DataOutputStream:

DataInputStream Method	Description
boolean readBoolean()	Reads a boolean input from the file
byte readByte()	Reads a byte input from the file
char readChar()	Reads a char input from the file
double readDouble()	Reads a double input from the file
float readFloat()	Reads a float input from the file
int readInt()	Reads a int input from the file
long readLong()	Reads a long input from the file
short readShort()	Reads a short input from the file

Figure 8.6 – DataInputStream Methods

DataOutputStream Method	Description
void writeBoolean(boolean v)	Writes a boolean output to the file
void writeByte(int v)	Writes a byte output to the file
void writeChar(int v)	Writes a char output to the file

3 Tips To Master Selenium Within 30 Days
http://tinyurl.com/3-Tips-For-Selenium

Free Webinars, Videos, and Live Trainings
http://tinyurl.com/Free-QTP-UFT-Selenium

Chapter 8
Utilizing Input and Output   (Part 2) Java 4 Selenium WebDriver

void writeDouble(double v)	Writes a double output to the file
void writeFloat(float v)	Writes a float output to the file
void writeInt(int v)	Writes a int output to the file
void writeLong(long v)	Writes a long output to the file
void writeShort(int v)	Writes a short output to the file

Figure 8.7 – DataOutputStream Methods

Standard Streams

Java provides support for standard I/O so a program receives input from a keyboard and produce output onto the computer monitor. A class called System within the java.lang package includes three standard stream variables: in, out, and err. System.in is an InputStream object while System.out and System.err are PrintStream objects. PrintStream allows formatted data to be written to an OutputStream. The following is a description of the standard streams:

Standard Stream	Description
Standard Input	(System.in) / By default the keyboard Standard Input controls where the program receives input
Standard Output	(System.out) / By default the console Standard Output controls where the program sends output
Standard Error	(System.err) / By default the console Standard Error used to output an error supplied by the program

Figure 8.8 – Standard Streams

File Input/Output

Files are stored and organized so they can be retrieved and accessed in a convenient manner. In Java, there are two packages "java.io.file and java.nio.fio" set aside for files. Package "java.nio.file" is the newer file system labeled NIO2 meaning "New Input/Output 2". NIO2 identifies interfaces and classes to access files, file attributes, and file systems.

Skype: rex.jones34
Twitter: @RexJonesII
Email: Rex.Jones@Test4Success.org
LinkedIn: https://www.linkedin.com/in/rexjones34

Chapter 8
Utilizing Input and Output   (Part 2) Java 4 Selenium WebDriver
Path

Most files are arranged in a hierarchical (known as tree) structure. The root node (i.e., C:\) is located at the top of the hierarchy followed by folders and files. All folders have the ability to include additional folders and files. A unique path identifies a specific resource (file or folder) within a tree. Therefore the path "C:\java4selenium\input_output\test.txt" indicates a file named "test" is located in a folder named "input_output" within another folder named "java4selenium". The following are common Path Interface methods for Java's file system:

Path Conversion

- toAbsolutePath ()
  Returns a Path object characterizing the absolute path

- toRealPath (LinkOption… options)
  Returns the real path of an existing file

- toUri ()
  Returns a URI to characterize this path

Retrieve Path Information

- getFileName ()
  Returns the name of the file or last element in the Path object

- getName (int index)
  Returns the Path element corresponding to the specified index

- getNameCount ()
  Returns the number of name elements in the path

3 Tips To Master Selenium Within 30 Days
http://tinyurl.com/3-Tips-For-Selenium

Free Webinars, Videos, and Live Trainings
http://tinyurl.com/Free-QTP-UFT-Selenium

Chapter 8
Utilizing Input and Output   (Part 2) Java 4 Selenium WebDriver

- getParent ()
  Returns the parent path or null

- getRoot ()
  Returns the path's root

- normalize ()
  Returns a path with redundant name elements eliminated

- resolve (Path other)
  Resolve the specified path against this path

- relativize (Path other)
  Constructs a relative path between this path and a specified path

- subPath (int beginIndex, int endIndex)
  Returns the subsequence of the Path indicated by starting and ending indices

- toString
  Returns the path's string representation

Files

Files can be created, deleted, moved, copied, and verified for existence. Both packages "java.io.file and java.nio.fio" include methods which read, write, and manipulate files and folders. The following are common methods within both packages for Java's file system:

Check Existence Methods

- exists(Path path, LinkOption... options)
  Tests if the resource exist

Skype: rex.jones34
Twitter: @RexJonesII
Email: Rex.Jones@Test4Success.org
LinkedIn: https://www.linkedin.com/in/rexjones34

Chapter 8
Utilizing Input and Output   (Part 2) Java 4 Selenium WebDriver

- notExists(Path path, LinkOption... options)
  Tests if the resource located by this path does not exist

Check Status Methods

- isDirectory (Path path, LinkOption… options)
  Tests if the resource is a directory

- isExecutable (Path path)
  Tests if the resource is executable

- isFile()
  Tests if the resource indicated by this abstract pathname is a normal resource

- isReadable (Path path)
  Tests if the resource is readable

- isSameFile (Path path, Path path2)
  Tests if two resources locate the same resource

- isWritable (Path path)
  Tests if the resource is writable

Copy Method

- copy (Path source, Path target, CopyOption… options)
  Copy the resource to a specified target

Create Method

- createFile (Path path, FileAttribute<?>... attrs)
  Creates a new and empty resource

3 Tips To Master Selenium Within 30 Days
http://tinyurl.com/3-Tips-For-Selenium

Free Webinars, Videos, and Live Trainings
http://tinyurl.com/Free-QTP-UFT-Selenium

Chapter 8
Utilizing Input and Output   (Part 2) Java 4 Selenium WebDriver
Delete Method

- Delete (Path path)
  Deletes the resource

Note: Folders must be empty before it can be deleted

Directory Methods

- list ()
  Returns an array of strings naming the resources and directories in the directory indicated by this abstract pathname

- listFiles ()
  Returns an array of abstract pathnames indicating the files in the directory indicated by this abstract pathname

Move Method

- move (Path source, Path target, CopyOption... options)
  Move or rename the resource to a target

Read Methods

- readAllBytes (Path path)
  Reads all the bytes from the resource

- readAllLines (Path path, Charset cs)
  Read all lines from the resource

Space Methods

- length ()
  Returns the length of the resource indicated by this abstract pathname

- getFreeSpace ()
  Returns the number of unallocated bytes in the partition named by this abstract

Skype: rex.jones34
Twitter: @RexJonesII
Email: Rex.Jones@Test4Success.org
LinkedIn: https://www.linkedin.com/in/rexjones34

Chapter 8
Utilizing Input and Output   (Part 2) Java 4 Selenium WebDriver
    pathname

- getTotalSpace ()
  Returns the size of the partition named by this abstract pathname

- getUsableSpace ()
  Returns the number of bytes available to this virtual machine on the partition named
  by this abstract pathname

Write Methods

- write (Path path, byte[] bytes, OpenOption... options)
  Writes bytes to the resource

- write (Path path, Iterable<? extends CharSequence> lines Charset cs, OpenOption...
  options)
  Write lines of text to the resource

Conclusion

Java is a popular object-oriented programming (OOP) language centered around objects. The goal of "*Part 2 – Java 4 Selenium WebDriver*" was to provide deep concepts of Java. One of the benefits of Java is the ability to reuse code. The following are take-away topics from this book:

Classes: A class is a template for objects which contains data and code that operates on the data.

Objects: Objects are the foundation to object-oriented programming. It consists of two characteristics: state and behavior. State identifies the object and behavior represent the actions of the object.

Methods: A method is a block of code that perform a specific task.

Inheritance: Inheritance is an OOP hierarchical concept which allows reusable code and objects to be extended.

Encapsulation: Encapsulation is an OOP concept where a class encapsulates code and data for protection.

Polymorphism: Polymorphism is an OOP concept that allows multiple methods to utilize one interface.

Package: A package is a collection of related classes.

Interface: An interface is a collection of related methods.

Error: An error is an unavoidable problem in a program.

Exceptions: An exception is an error that occurs at runtime

Skype: rex.jones34
Twitter: @RexJonesII
Email: Rex.Jones@Test4Success.org
LinkedIn: https://www.linkedin.com/in/rexjones34

Conclusion   (Part 2) Java 4 Selenium WebDriver

<u>Debugging</u>: Debugging is the process of detecting and removing unexpected conditions from the program.

3 Tips To Master Selenium Within 30 Days
http://tinyurl.com/3-Tips-For-Selenium

Free Webinars, Videos, and Live Trainings
http://tinyurl.com/Free-QTP-UFT-Selenium

Resources

1. Beginning Java® Programming
   The Object-Oriented Approach
   Bart Baesens, Aimée Backiel, Seppe vanden Broucke

2. Java A Beginner's Guide Sixth Edition
   Create, Compile, and Run Java Programs Today
   Herbert Schildt

3. ORACLE Java Documentation
   The Java ™ Tutorials
   https://docs.oracle.com/javase/tutorial/java/javaOO/returnvalue.html
   https://docs.oracle.com/javase/7/docs/api/
   https://docs.oracle.com/javase/7/docs/api/java/io/package-summary.html#package_description

4. Program Creek
   http://www.programcreek.com/2009/02/diagram-for-hierarchy-of-exception-classes/

5. TIOBE
   http://www.tiobe.com/tiobe_index

6. Dictionary.com
   http://www.dictionary.com/browse/object?s=t
   http://www.dictionary.com/browse/annotation?s=t

Skype: rex.jones34
Twitter: @RexJonesII
Email: Rex.Jones@Test4Success.org
LinkedIn: https://www.linkedin.com/in/rexjones34

Download PDF Version

The PDF Version of this book is available to you at the following link.

http://tinyurl.com/P2-Java-4-Selenium-WebDriver

If the book was helpful, can you leave a favorable review?

http://tinyurl.com/Review-Part-2-Java-4-Selenium

Thanks in advance,

Rex Allen Jones II

3 Tips To Master Selenium Within 30 Days
http://tinyurl.com/3-Tips-For-Selenium

Free Webinars, Videos, and Live Trainings
http://tinyurl.com/Free-QTP-UFT-Selenium

Books by Rex Jones II

www.tinyurl.com/Rex-Allen-Jones-books

1. **Free Book** Absolute Beginner
   (Part 1) You Must Learn VBScript for QTP/UFT
   Don't Ignore The Language For Functional Automation Testing

2. (Part 2) You Must Learn VBScript for QTP/UFT
   Don't Ignore The Language For Functional Automation Testing

3. **Free Book** Absolute Beginner
   (Part 1) Java 4 Selenium WebDriver
   Come Learn How To Program For Automation Testing

4. (Part 2) Java 4 Selenium WebDriver
   Come Learn How To Program For Automation Testing

5. **Free Book** Absolute Beginner
   (Part 1) Selenium WebDriver for Functional Automation Testing
   Your Beginners Guide

6. Getting Started With TestNG
   A Java Test Framework

Skype: rex.jones34
Twitter: @RexJonesII
Email: Rex.Jones@Test4Success.org
LinkedIn: https://www.linkedin.com/in/rexjones34

Books by Rex Jones II   (Part 2) Java 4 Selenium WebDriver

3 Tips To Master Selenium Within 30 Days
http://tinyurl.com/3-Tips-For-Selenium

Free Webinars, Videos, and Live Trainings
http://tinyurl.com/Free-QTP-UFT-Selenium

Sign Up To Receive

1. 3 Tips To Master Selenium Within 30 Days
   http://tinyurl.com/3-Tips-For-Selenium

2. 3 Tips To Master QTP/UFT Within 30 Days
   http://tinyurl.com/3-Tips-For-QTP-UFT

3. Free Webinars, Videos, and Live Trainings
   http://tinyurl.com/Free-QTP-UFT-Selenium

Skype: rex.jones34
Twitter: @RexJonesII
Email: Rex.Jones@Test4Success.org
LinkedIn: https://www.linkedin.com/in/rexjones34

www.ingramcontent.com/pod-product-compliance
Lightning Source LLC
La Vergne TN
LVHW062319060326
832902LV00013B/2302